FRANCE ON THE
EVE OF REVOLUTION

MAJOR ISSUES IN HISTORY

Editor
C. WARREN HOLLISTER
University of California, Santa Barbara

William F. Church: *The Impact of Absolutism in France: National Experience under Richelieu, Mazarin, and Louis XIV*

Robert O. Collins: *The Partition of Africa: Illusion or Necessity*

J. B. Conacher: *The Emergence of Parliamentary Democracy in Britain in the Nineteenth Century*

Gerald D. Feldman: *German War Aims, 1914-1918: The Development of an Historical Debate*

Frank J. Frost: *Democracy and the Athenians*

Paul Hauben: *The Spanish Inquisition*

Bennett D. Hill: *Church and State in the Middle Ages*

Boyd H. Hill: *The Rise of the First Reich: Germany in the Tenth Century*

C. Warren Hollister: *The Impact of the Norman Conquest*

C. Warren Hollister: *The Twelfth-Century Renaissance*

Thomas M. Jones: *The Becket Controversy*

Tom B. Jones: *The Sumerian Problem*

Jeffry Kaplow: *France on the Eve of Revolution*

Archibald Lewis: *Islamic World and the West*

Anthony Molho: *Social and Economic Foundations of the Italian Renaissance*

E. W. Monter: *European Witchcraft*

Donald Queller: *The Latin Conquest of Constantinople*

Joachim Remak: *The First World War: Causes, Conduct, Consequences*

Jeffrey Russell: *Medieval Religious Dissent*

Max Salvadori: *European Liberalism*

Arthur J. Slavin: *Humanism, Reform, and Reformation*

W. Warren Wagar: *The Idea of Progress Since the Renaissance*

Bertie Wilkinson: *The Creation of the Medieval Parliament*

L. Pearce Williams: *Relativity Theory: Its Origins and Impact on Modern Thought*

Roger L. Williams: *The Commune of Paris, 1871*

FRANCE ON THE EVE OF REVOLUTION:

A Book of Readings

EDITED BY
Jeffry Kaplow

John Wiley & Sons, Inc.
New York · London · Sydney · Toronto

Library of Congress Catalogue Card Number: 79–142716

Cloth: ISBN 0-417-45796-5   Paper: ISBN 0-471-45797-3

Printed in the United States of America

10 9 8 7 6 5 4 3 2 1

SERIES PREFACE

The reading program in a history survey course traditionally has consisted of a large two-volume textbook and, perhaps, a book of readings. This simple reading program requires few decisions and little imagination on the instructor's part, and tends to encourage in the student the virtue of careful memorization. Such programs are by no means things of the past, but they certainly do not represent the wave of the future.

The reading program in survey courses at many colleges and universities today is far more complex. At the risk of over-simplification, and allowing for many exceptions and overlaps, it can be divided into four categories: (1) textbook, (2) original source readings, (3) specialized historical essays and interpretive studies, and (4) historical problems.

After obtaining an overview of the course subject matter (textbook), sampling the original sources, and being exposed to selective examples of excellent modern historical writing (historical essays), the student can turn to the crucial task of weighing various possible interpretations of major historical issues. It is at this point that memory gives way to creative critical thought. The "problems approach," in other words, is the intellectual climax of a thoughtfully conceived reading program and is, indeed, the most characteristic of all approaches to historical pedagogy among the newer generation of college and university teachers.

The historical problems books currently available are many and varied. Why add to this information explosion? Because the Wiley Major Issues Series constitutes an endeavor to produce something new that will respond to pedagogical needs thus far unmet. First, it is a series of individual volumes—one per problem. Many good teachers would much prefer to select their own historical issues rather than be tied to an inflexible sequence of issues imposed by a publisher and bound together between two covers. Second, the Wiley Major Issues Series is based on the idea of approaching the significant problems of history through a deft interweaving of primary sources and secondary analysis, fused together by the skill of a scholar-editor. It is felt that the essence of a historical issue cannot be satisfactorily probed either by placing a body of undigested source materials into the hands of inexperienced students or by limiting these students to the controversial literature of modern scholars who debate the meaning of sources the student never sees. This series approaches historical problems by exposing students to both the finest historical thinking on the issue and some of the evidence on which this thinking is based. This synthetic approach should prove far more fruitful than either the raw-source approach or the exclusively second-hand approach, for it combines the advantages— and avoids the serious disadvantages—of both.

Finally, the editors of the individual volumes in the Major Issues Series have been chosen from among the ablest scholars in their fields. Rather than faceless referees, they are historians who know their issues from the inside and, in most instances, have themselves contributed significantly to the relevant scholarly literature. It has been the editorial policy of this series to permit the editor-scholars of the individual volumes the widest possible latitude both in formulating their topics and in organizing their materials. Their scholarly competence has been unquestioningly respected; they have been encouraged to approach the problems as they see fit. The titles and themes of the series volumes have been suggested in nearly every case by the scholar-editors themselves. The criteria have been (1) that the issue be of relevance to undergraduate lecture courses in history, and (2) that it be an issue which the scholar-editor knows thoroughly and in which he has done creative work. And, in general, the second criterion has been given precedence over the first. In short, the question "What are the significant historical issues today?" has been answered not by general editors or sales departments but by the scholar-teachers who are responsible for these volumes.

University of California,   *C. Warren Hollister*
Santa Barbara

PREFACE

The objective of this book is to introduce students to some of the problems that beset eighteenth century France and led, in 1789, to the outbreak of the Revolution. The coverage is selective. Some readers will probably regret the absence of a section devoted to the clergy or to the attempts made to reform an inadequate state administration, to name only two topics dear to earlier historians. I decided to illustrate in somewhat greater detail the material conditions, life styles, and ways of thought of the major parties to the Revolution—nobility, bourgeoisie, urban workers, and peasants—hoping to clarify the points of conflict that were latent in French society on the eve of the Revolution. To prevent the charge that I believe in immanence in history, let me say that the subject under study in this book has to do with the causes of the Revolution. The eighteenth century may be worthy of study for other reasons, but here it is taken as prelude to the great changes that marked its end.

Instead of a single long introduction, I have written a few words at the beginning of each section to explain the historical context of the documents. My choice of readings emphasizes the importance of social history, that is, of the relationships and conflicts that grow up among great numbers of men as they perform the task of creating a society suitable to their needs, rather than of the activities of statesmen and diplomats alone. I believe that the French Revolution occurred because an increasingly self-conscious bourgeoisie needed power, that is, control of the state apparatus, in order to develop further. But the Revolution could not have taken place without the participation of urban wage carners and peasants, men and women who were moved to action by hunger and the fear that they might find themselves unable to make a living—even by the fear that there was an active conspiracy afoot directed toward achieving that end. The will to power, on the one hand, and misery and the credulous fear to which it gave rise, on the other hand, were the elements whose complementary actions gave the period its particular configuration.

Finally, it will be evident that the concerns implicit in these documents are not limited to eighteenth century France. They have much greater implications. For instance, the ways in which the nobility

sought to preserve its power and to create a rationale for its pre-
eminent place in society at a time when its traditional functions had
been all but lost will point to questions that may be asked about ruling
classes in any society—or at least in every European society before
the Industrial Revolution. Again, the study of the master–servant
relationship in the guilds may lead us to pose questions about hierarchical social relations in general—in the family as well as in the
workshop, in the contemporary world as well as in the eighteenth
century. To seek to imbue historical studies with relevance to our
own time in a gratuitous manner is a useless (and ultimately self-
defeating) exercise because it both obscures our vision of the past
and hinders our actions in the present. But history does have relevance
on a higher level of abstraction, insofar as it enables us to study the
mechanisms of change in human society: (1) to ask how and why we
got where we are today and (2) to ask how we get to where we want to
go tomorrow. The past teaches us no lessons, but it (or history, which
is its written form) may help us to develop a method for understanding
the present and shaping the future. In my view, relevance can have no
other meaning.

JEFFRY KAPLOW

CONTENTS

PART IV

The Urban Workers and the Poor

PART V

The Peasantry

PART VI

Cahiers de Doléances

FRANCE ON THE
EVE OF REVOLUTION

I   THE GENERAL SITUATION

Following the suggestion of Alexis de Tocqueville in his *Old Regime and the Revolution* (1856), historians have habitually made much of the increasing prosperity of eighteenth century France. The Revolution has been called a crisis of rising expectations because of the evidence that conditions in France had been inproving more or less steadily in the fifty years before 1789. Although this is true in one sense, it does not tell the whole story.

The question is: to what conditions do we refer? Measured from a quantitative point of view in regard to total production or overseas trade (to take only two examples), the economy was expanding both absolutely and in relation to a rapidly growing population. There was definitely a connection between the development and increase of new forms of bourgeois (but not necessarily capitalist) wealth and the subjective desire of certain bourgeois to assert their power by taking over the reins of government. However, for the great mass of the people still laboring in the toils of archaic socioeconomic structures, this prosperity was likely to be a chimera, or, at the very least, it did not greatly change their conditions of work or life. Their rebellion in 1789 was still directed against the traditional enemies of famine, under-employment, and the abuses of an administration more concerned with collecting taxes than in assuming responsibility for a nation's survival.

1 FROM M. Moheau
Recherches et Considérations sur la Population en France

Antoine-Jean-Baptiste-Robert Auget, Baron de Montyon (1733–1820), who wrote under the name of Moheau, was one of the earliest and most important French demographers. His research was based on first-hand experience when he was successively intendant of Auvergne, Provence and the generality of La Rochelle in the 1760s and 1770s. As a man who equated population growth with prosperity, he argued (correctly, as later research has shown) that there had been an increase in the number of Frenchmen, although at the same time he was conscious of the miseries still faced by most of them. Montyon emphasized that the poor, both rural and urban, were much better housed, clothed, and fed than ever before. Everything being relative, he was probably right. The belief in measured progress implicit in the following reading is the attitude of a man imbued with the ideas of the Enlightenment. He had recently seen "hunger transformed into passion," but knew that in the long run famines were no longer as terrible or as murderous as they had once been. French population had grown from twenty to twenty-six millions in the course of the eighteenth century, an increase of approximately thirty percent—largely attributable to a dramatic decrease in the death rate. Epidemic disease and famine, although far from absent, no longer worked hand in hand as a mortal scourge. Fewer deaths meant that more people lived to raise a family and that their children were born healthier and were more likely to survive to adulthood, with the snowballing effect that we call a population explosion. In Europe the year 1750 generally marked the dividing line between the old and new demographic regimes.

Montyon also alluded to the difficulties of food distribution, claiming that substantial changes had recently been made in patterns of regional isolation. He was perhaps too optimistic. Although numerous roads were built during the eighteenth century, they did not automatically supply hard-pressed areas with food. Peasants' suspicion and distrust of distant places and peoples—distance being measured relative to the amount of ground a peasant may have covered in a life time's travel, which was often not a great deal—and the fear of being caught short, together with singularly inept governmental policies that failed to take into consideration the problems of local particularism militated against the development of an integrated national economy. The attempts in the 1760s and 1770s to free the grain trade were basically failures, since they did little to protect people from starvation. Although at the same time the attempts against the grain trade excited popular wrath against what was seen as a series of plots to deprive Jacques Bonhomme and Père Duchesne, the peasant and

SOURCE. M. Moheau, Recherches et Considérations sur la Population en France (Paris, Chez Mourard, 1778), pp. 260–268. Translated for this volume by Susan Kaplow.

3

*the artisan, of their food. It is against this background that the riots of the Great Fear
and the early revolutionary journées of 1789 must be studied.*

*The remarks made in this selection about improvements in agricultural technique
and the cultivation of land are true, but should not be taken to indicate the existence
of anything like an agricultural revolution on the English model. One of the unique
characteristics of postrevolutionary France is the extent to which small holdings
survived and were consolidated in the midst of capitalist industrialization. Indeed,
the special features of French industrial capitalism are at least partially attributable
to the maintenance of peasant proprietors on the land throughout the nineteenth
century and into the twentieth. As we shall see, the peasant, in particular the small
holder, had many problems in the old regime, but the constant threat of having his
land taken away from him for purposes of large-scale capitalist development was not·
one of them.*

For nearly six thousand years, man has complained of his fate;
and for six thousand years he has been right to do so. An existence of
a small number of years, a double portion of this existence taken up
by childhood and old age—two extremes destined to suffering and
pains; almost a third of life absorbed by sleep, which is neither life
nor death; a great part of the time necessarily sacrificed to other
human needs; illnesses and woes often torment us for years.

Of the little time remaining to us, the greatest part is used up in
painful labors, which physical necessity, customs, or conventions
make necessary. We scarcely have time to enjoy being alive. Not
satisfied with deploring these evils, necessary and inevitable consequences of the human condition, we may speculate on the growth
or decline in the number of men, by an appraisal of their well-being
compared to that of former times. We must examine their situation
with regard to their primary needs, shelter, clothing and food.

If one passes through the cities of France, one finds no comparison
between the old and the new dwellings. In all the provinces, the old
settlements and the new cities seem to be of two different countries.
The modern houses are without doubt bigger, more comfortable, and
healthier than those they have supplanted.

If we turn our attention to the houses of the countryside, we find
signs of misery everywhere. But, although few vestiges of the old
lodgings of the poor remain, one can see that fewer are made of
mud, that the new ones are less close together and better ventilated,

that well-situated places of habitation have become increasingly populated, while the others have become less so. Thus we find improvement in the location and form of residences.

In regard to clothing, we shall only consider the poor, since they make up the majority of the nation. The French peasant is badly dressed, and the rags that cover his nakedness afford him little protection against the rigors of the seasons. Nevertheless, it seems that his state in the matter of clothing is less deplorable than in former times.

For a poor man, clothing is not a luxury but an essential defense against the cold. Linen, worn by many peasants, does not protect them sufficiently against the severity of the seasons. But in recent years this type of apparel has become less frequent, and many more peasants are dressed in wool.

This is easily proven. For it is a certainty that for some time a greater quantity of coarse woollen cloth has been produced in the realm. As this cloth is not exported, it obviously serves to clothe a greater number of Frenchmen. The attire of the poor is certainly better than that which covered him before underwear was known and had come into general use. Scabs and tenia and all the skin diseases caused by lack of cleanliness used to be common only because of the lack of underwear.

But clothing and shelter are much less important than food. This latter is the subject of greatest interest, the one to which all others are subordinate. And with regard to it, humanity has recently been cruelly mistreated. Witness of calamity, I have seen the latest epoch of misery; I have seen hunger transformed into passion, the inhabitants of a region without a harvest wander, led astray by suffering and deprived of everything, envy the fate of domestic animals, lie down in a meadow to eat grass, and share the food of wild beasts.

But if these horrors were confined to a small area, calamity has been general. From one end of the kingdom to the other, a national cry rose up against the lack of food, and there is almost no town or province whose food supply has not been threatened.[1]

However great these misfortunes, it seems unlikely that they were less in other times, and the traces which they have left indicate that

---

[1]Moheau is no doubt referring to the food shortages of 1775, which gave rise to bread riots in several places, notably in the Paris region. See George Rudé, "The Bread Riots of May 1775," in J. Kaplow (ed.), *New Perspectives on the French Revolution* (New York, 1965), pp. 191–210.

the famines of previous centuries were more frequent, more wide-spread, and more terrible.

Before means of communication had been established, each region closed in by mountains, ravines, streams, and rivers lived solely from its own production and could not get supplies from neighboring areas nor furnish them any. It is probable that at that time less grain was cultivated because any surplus could not be sold.

When several lean years followed one another, the stores of previous years were insufficient to prevent misfortune, and the evil was without remedy. Recourse to the throne was neither easy nor the usual practice, and the unfortunates died without help.

The losses were little known but more numerous. Historians have not been overly careful in transmitting to us these misfortunes of the people. Yet we see that in the tenth century there were ten famines; in the eleventh, twenty-six; in the twelfth, two; in the fourteenth, four; in the fifteenth, seven; in the sixteenth, six. And these famines were not the ordinary scarcities: there were some during which the dead were disinterred and human flesh was sold.

As to the eating habits of the people, we have been able to observe that in several provinces or regions in which the inhabitants formerly ate bread made of buckwheat, barley, or rye flour, the type of bread eaten has now improved.

We have been unable to determine if a greater number of people eat meat. But certainly, there are many who drink wine, an excellent beverage for the poor, not only because it is nourishing, but also because it is a very good antiputrefactive.

After looking at these primary needs, essential bases of the people's well-being, we can evaluate this well-being by other factors. If we examine the rights and possessions of the poor, we find that again their lot has improved. It is not in the cities alone that the inhabitants enjoy constant daylight, where the streets are paved, the water better or less badly distributed and carried than in former times.

Even in the countryside, the inhabitants have many new possessions and rights. A road, a bridge, a dyke are all public properties from which the most humble citizen profits, and one cannot deny that in this respect our well-being has increased.

It is possible that some families or some places have lost out. But there is no province in France where dwellings are more unhealthy, communications less established, and life more difficult than fifty years ago.

We are far from concluding from these observations that the state of the people in France is as happy as it might be; nor is it what humanity demands, and it is not even equal to that of several of our neighbors. But we believe that the poverty of the people is several degrees less than before. And since this life-destroying plague, is less active today, we can presume that there is a large population.

The growth of the French population is confirmed if we judge the number of inhabitants by their work. In previous centuries, crafts were unknown to us, but today we can perhaps count one hundred artisans for every one in olden times.

All labor was formerly directed toward cultivation of the soil, and there were almost as many farmers as inhabitants. But if there existed a greater number of farmers than today, agriculture must have been more widespread. Yet it is beyond doubt that France has never been better cultivated than at the present moment.

Consult the charters, the ancient land titles, the rent of rolls the seigneurs in every region; you will see that the lands that now provide grain used to be woodlands, swamps, or meadows. Not only has a great amount of land been cleared or drained, but old cultivated land is better today. About this, the old people of the countryside are obliged to agree.

An even more remarkable point concerning population is that the very culture that requires the greatest number of hands is the one whose progress is the most marked. In the majority of provinces where the vine is cultivated, the last fifty years have seen a doubling in the growth of this product; in several regions, it has quintupled. Certainly, then, there existed formerly fewer farmers. And as farming was the universal profession of the nation, it follows that there existed fewer inhabitants.

Thus, if one considers the physical, moral, of political causes that influence the progress or decadence of the population, or if one examines the factors that prove its strength or weakness, one must recognize that the population of the realm has grown considerably.

Then, coming back to our usual method, we may submit this proposition to statistical scrutiny. If we compare the number of births to the number of deaths, or the number of births to those provided by censuses at diverse eras, our research will shed more new light on our proposition.

It has already been recognized that population is the difference between the number of births and the number of deaths. These gains and losses of the nation form the balance that determines its condition; and it is an established fact that in France the number of births is superior to the number of deaths.

This difference is less marked in the cities, because many people who die in the cities were not born there. But in the countryside, due to the opposite effect, the increase in population is enormous and can be as high as one-fourth more. For the entire kingdom, there are annually one-seventh more births than deaths.

It is true that from this surplus about 20,000 births must be deducted to take account of emigration. But losses of this type are negligible and the surplus always remains in about the same proportion.

This type of argument would be conclusive if the inequality in the number of deaths from one year to another did not diminish the confidence one can have in its basis. But even if one cannot use it to ascertain the rate of population growth, there is evident, nevertheless, a certainty that there is some annual growth.

2 FROM   Dupuy and Charvol (eds.)
Journal d'un Curé de Campagne

There had indeed been progress along many fronts. Fewer people than before died of epidemic diseases and famine after 1750. The "power of death" was diminishing in the sense that men might expect to live longer and to enjoy a higher standard of physical comfort (that is, freedom from disease). The great menace of infant mortality began to lose some of its force. With the change in the demographic regime, attitudes might be revised. There was now more room for optimism and confidence that the world might yet be set right. The development of a popularly held "idea of progress" is a possibility that ought not to be neglected in attempting to understand the intellectual and emotional origins of the French Revolution.

On the other hand, old habits of mind die hard. They probably live longest among those people who are most subject to the threats and who are least sophistcated in their ways of thought. It would be a mistake to suppose that French peasants and urban workers in the old regime were ever free of these age-old fears. It is for this reason that I have included the following descriptions of plague and famine which were, after all, the inspiration of those fears. Both selections emphasize the acceptance of one's fate in the spirit of Christian humility. The doctor and the priest

SOURCE. Dupuy and Charvot (eds.), "Journal d'un curé de campagne (1712–1765)," in *Annales de Bretagne*, V (1889–1890), pp. 419–423. Translated for this volume by Susan Kaplow.

seem to agree that there is a certain fatality to the events that beset them. God is angry with his people, and so he sends them this visitation. The only thing to do is to take the lesson, to go and sin no more. There is strong evidence to suggest that this psychology of acceptance was widespread throughout the eighteenth century, and no-where more so than among the menu peuple, *although it was not exclusive to them.*

Bertrand suggests that the plague dehumanized as well as killed. So terrible were conditions in Marseilles that parents turned sick children out into the streets rather than run the risk of contagion by caring for them. In reality this is only one aspect of a much more common situation. In an era of enormous infant mortality, it was not possible for parents to place the same value on children as we do today. Infants were abandoned or sent to foundling homes in great numbers, most often because it was economically impossible to rear them. Children who grew up at home often went out to work at an early age—whether in the father's workshop, in someone else's employ, or as an errand boy in the streets was a matter of circumstance. The effect of all this on the family is a matter of speculation. That loyalty and respect were due the parents by the children seems clear, but parents' duties toward their offspring are less certain. There was a belief in the necessity of upholding family honor, and even humble parents sometimes took the initiative of having an errant child jailed on a royal order, lest he or she bring disgrace on the name. Such ties of affection as might have bound individuals together under these difficult conditions are an unknown quantity.

The following is a note written by the Abbé Lefeuvre, curé of Saint Mars du Désert, relating the rigors of the winter of 1709. The account was written on paper normally destined to serve as the parish register of births, marriages, and deaths.

This year 1709 is too remarkable not to leave its memory to posterity, and since the liberality of the tax farmers [*maltôtiers*—a pejorative word designating the employees of the General Farm] has given us more paper than necessary for our registers, I can do no better than to put my little remarks on what remains of the paper, the more so as it [i.e., the register] ought never to be destroyed because it cost us so much and, if we happen to lose it, it would be necessary to have recourse to people who, only too happy to have the opportunity, would not fail to sell dear that which cost them nothing, but for which they made us pay a great deal.

After this small preamble, I say then that this year is remarkable not for some good thing, but on account of I know not how many misfortunes that have befallen us all at once.

I do not speak of a long and cruel war that afflicted France, and in which the country that had been accustomed to dictate to other nations found herself obliged in her turn to be dictated to by her conquerors. Beaten time and time again, we have seen our enemies live off our country, take our cities, win victories without luck coming over to our side: the result being that the people, weighted down by all kinds of new taxes, complained bitterly, while waiting for divine goodness to remove from our shoulders this horrible burden of war.

But the sins of men had gone so far that God's justice was not satisfied with war; we are punished in an even more tangible way, through the sterility of the land caused by a horrid winter whose unfortunate effects I am going to describe. This winter was so violent that living men could not remember one like it, not so much from the point of view of its duration as from its several recurrences and the rigor of its cold.

The cold began to be felt at the end of October 1708, on the evening of the Feast of the Apostles Saint Simon and Jude, October 28, 1708. The wind shifted to the north, the rain that had been falling all day long turned into ice and snow, and one saw therein a warning of what was to happen later on because the snow, having frozen in the trees, weighed on them so heavily that branches as heavy as men were seen to succumb under the burden and fall to the ground, and I am an eyewitness that most of the oak trees of the parish were badly damaged.

This cold lasted only seven or eight days, and the rest of the year passed mildly enough. The next year began in the same way, but not for long, since on the evening of January 6 the wind, having once again shifted to the north, became so cold that there was ice everywhere the next morning. Another sign of the cold's bitterness is that the Loire River, which usually carries pieces of ice about in it for seven to eight days before freezing over, froze on the second day of the cold spell. The cold increased to such an extent that carts and carriages could pass over the river without fear.

Nothing withstood this cold; many men died of it, but to tell the truth not in the immediate vicinity; almost no birds remained; partridge were taken by hand or were found dead, together with other game, either as a result of the cold or because the ground was always covered with snow. But if only that had been the greatest evil! Wheat died and vines dried up; none of the large trees, neither the oaks nor the fruit trees, could withstand it; and the chestnut and walnut trees were especially ill treated. When one had confidence to venture out, one could hear the oaks breaking apart, and I have seen some open to a width of three fingers from top to bottom.

Finally, after three weeks of this cold, which increased continually, the thaw came. Its sad effects were not yet known. Work was begun on the vines in the usual manner, but this soon became impossible because the cold began again at the start of Lent toward the middle of February and lasted fifteen days in the same violent manner. The sun, however, was stronger and made the cold more bearable to men during the day, but much more damaging to what remained of the produce of the earth, which could not resist the terrible nights that caused almost everything to die, so that it was scarcely possible to gather enough to provide for next year's seed.

Never were we more surprised than when, after this last cold spell, we saw the earth completely bare and the seed dead. We decided to look at the bud of the vine, which we found to be black, without any sap, and, in fact, it had grown only one tenth as much as usual; and this was only at the base so that the following year it was necessary to cut the vines all off at ground level, not knowing whether they would ever grow again.

Wheat was soon at 28 livres the *septier*, and wine at 100 francs the *pipe*[1], and money scarcer than ever. It was hardly possible even for those who knew how, to find money, when there wasn't any. The number of poor people increased incredibly because the continuing rains of the previous year, 1708, had been very bad and had damaged the grain crops by filling them with tares. The poor of the countryside were destitute of any aid, no longer possessing a cabbage or a leek in their gardens, so they crowded into the cities to take part in the liberalities of the inhabitants, which were very considerable, at least in Nantes—for I cannot speak of other cities.

But they were soon begrudged the only help they had. They were forced, by the threat of great penalties, to return to their homes, and there soon appeared the most beautiful edicts in the world to help them, which, however, served only to increase their misfortune. Each parish was supposed to feed its own poor; but for this it would have been necessary for the poor to feed the poor. So these lovely edicts were without effect, and the only way to help the poor, by decreasing the taxes with which they were burdened, was never put into practice. On the contrary, they were increased . . . .

But people did not lose courage; the earth was replanted with

---

[1] It is difficult to give precise modern equivalents of the *septier* and the *pipe*, as they varied from place to place. In Paris, the *septier* contained 256 liters and the *pipe*, 3072 liters.

oats and barley, which gave good yields and were of great help. In the month of April, buckwheat was planted, which turned out well; then the true planting season came, and so great a quantity was sown that the Nantes bushel was worth up to thirty sous. This was the only hope for that year. Thus people who normally ate bread made of wheat and rye were happy to have bread made of oats and buckwheat.

Toward the time of the Feast of Saint John the Baptist [June 24] a crowning misfortune came to pass. The islands of the Loire promised an abundant harvest, but we were surprised when, at the moment we least expected it, the waters swelled so furiously and so high that everything was submerged. How disappointing it is to see such lovely promises vanish in a moment! The water remained high for a long time before ebbing, and there were three successive waves of this nature, so that nothing could be gathered all along the Loire, which fact much increased the misery that was already so great.

Finally, harvest time came, but people remained idle because there was practically nothing to harvest. What could be was collected, so as to be able at least to replant the land the following year, and that was all that could be done. The time came for the wine harvest, which was even less abundant than the grain harvest, for there was none at all. People cut the vines in this year 1710 without knowing what would become of them. It is not necessary to describe here the misery in which the people found themselves: it can be seen well enough from what has already been said.

Such were the two years 1709 and 1710, but no doubt for our own good and for the good of those who must follow us. For our own good because these are punishments arising from the bad use we have made of the produce of the soil, and for the good of those who will succeed us because it is a good lesson which teaches us to receive what God gives us with all kinds of thanksgiving, as Saint Paul says. May it please the Lord that we shall all profit from it!

3 FROM   *Bertrand*
A Historical Relation of the Plague at Marseilles in the
Year 1720

This is a contemporary account of the bubonic plague epidemic that raged in Marseilles from May to December 1720, written by Bertrand, one of the attending physicians. It would be instructive to compare this description to Defoe's Journal of the Plague Year (1722) concerning the calamities that befell London in 1665.

STATE OF THE CITY

Hitherto the city had appeared deserted—It seemed as if all the inhabitants had quitted it, and not a soul remained there. This solitude was yet more supportable than the spectacle of such a number of sick and dead as now in a few days filled all the streets and public places. Many causes combined to produce an effect so horrible.

The hospitals, as we have already remarked, were wholly inadequate to the reception of such numbers—the poor, thus left without a retreat, and destitute of every thing at home, descended into the streets, either to excite the charity of their neighbours, or in the faint hope of finding a refuge in the hospital. Many persons not in a state of want, but who lived alone, without a family, without a servant, seeing themselves likely to perish, deprived of all succour, came alike into the streets, in hopes to find there what they must expect in vain at home. The same was the case with those who remained the last of a family—Left alone, after having given succour to the rest, their only hope was in exposing themselves in such a state of suffering to the vicissitudes of the weather in the open air.

Another description of unhappy victims, and whose fate was the most deplorable of all, was—will it be believed?—ought I to relate it?—The children of parents in whom fear of the evil had stifled every sentiment of nature. Inhumanly turned into the streets with

SOURCE. Anne Plumptre (translator), *A Historical Relation of the Plague at Marseilles in the year 1720 . . . translated from the French Manuscript of Mons. Bertrand, Physician at Marseilles* (London, Joseph Mawman, 1805), 122–136, 234–247.

nothing but miserable rags to cover them, they wandered about help-
less and forlorn, while the parents, by this barbarity, became the
murderers of those to whom not long before they boasted to have
given life. All these poor wretches brought nothing with them into
the street but a little pitcher, a porringer, and some wretched rag, such
as an old blanket, or something similar, to cover them. With this
miserable equipage they crawled on as far as they could. Some fell
after a few steps, exhausted by such an effort—others, stopping to
rest continually, by this means got at length to the place they
sought.—They laid down on the threshold of a door, or on a stone
bench before some shop, or under the shelter of the awning before it.
But even these sad asylums were soon denied them. Every one feared
the approach of a person infected, and drove them from their houses,
throwing dirty water or the lees of wine on the threshold and on the
pavement to prevent their remaining there. Thus, driven from the
street, they had no resource but to seek refuge in the squares and
market-places.

It was there that the heart and senses were wholly overpowered.
He must indeed have been lost to every sentiment of humanity who
could behold unmoved so many miserable figures, perhaps two
hundred at a time, deprived of every comfort, and sinking under the
weight of the most malignant of all diseases, exposed, without any
means of procuring an alleviation of their sufferings, alike to the
scorching heat of the sun and to the chillness of the night air. Death
was painted on every face, though in different forms and colours. One
was pale and cadaverous—another furiously red—another wan and
livid—another yellow—another violet. Some with eyes sunk and
hollow—others with eyes sparkling with fever—some with looks faint
and languishing—others wild and distracted; but all with an air of
terror and despondency which rendered them scarcely cognizable. . . .

Nor let it be supposed that this frightful spectacle was confined to
one place alone—it was the same in all. The Course, the gayest place
in the town, the great promenade of the principal company, where
the ladies usually appeared in all their splendor and elegance, ex-
hibited one of the most frightful among these scenes. Seeking shelter
under the shade of the trees from the sun, by which they were burned
from without, and the fever that parched them within, they demanded
only a little water to allay their thirst; but from no one could it be
obtained—all charity was extinguished in every breast. These unhappy wretches sought the most public parts in which to expose their
misery; in hopes that, among the numbers accustomed to pass, some

one might be found whose heart would be touched with their sufferings—alas, in vain! all shun, all fly them. They must wait the arrival of a Turk or Infidel, who, like the Samaritan in the Gospel, may wash their wounds and administer to their woes—but Christians only pass, and, like the Priest and the Levite, while they pity their misfortunes, they pass without relieving them. Cruel and forlorn situation, which will for ever be a shame to Christiantiy!

But to see the acme of desolation and horrors collected in one point of view, we have only to cast our eyes upon the Rue Dauphine, which leads from the Course to the hospital of the convalescents. The last efforts of the sufferers were directed to this spot, in hopes of reaching the hospital and being admitted there. But if they did reach it, how few could be admitted; and, not having power to return, they laid down to breathe their last in this street. Let the reader imagine a street 1080 feet long, and 30 wide, covered for a long time with these miserable wretches, to a degree that no one could quit their houses without passing as it were over a heap of bodies, dead or dying. Who can describe the sufferings of such a situation, or the various attitudes of these expiring bodies, and the dismal cries and groans to be heard on all sides? Crowded together, they had scarcely so much room as the uneasy state occasioned by the disease demanded. Some died before they reached the hospital; others, through weakness, fell down in the kennel, and had not strength to crawl away from it—others, parched with thirst, sought to dip their tongues in the water, and expired in the effort—in short, that none of the horrors to be seen in Jerusalem might be wanting at Marseilles, mothers were seen expiring with their infants at their breasts. . . .

If the sight of the sick excited alternately sentiments of horror and compassion, that of the dead raised trouble and terror in every breast. All the streets were covered with them; such numbers fell every day, that it became a matter of the utmost embarrassment to provide for their interment. It was scarcely possible to find persons who would make graves, or remove the bodies; and those who could be prevailed on to undertake this melancholy office made an infamous traffic of it, removing only the remains of such as had left relations in a situation and with a disposition to pay them handsomely. It will easily be imagined that, in such circumstances, the number interred was very small. The dead, therefore, accumulated in such heaps, that the moment seemed to approach when their removal would become impracticable . . . it is not difficult to conceive what must have been the situation of a town, in which, perhaps, a thousand persons had died in a day for many days successively, to whom the streets and public places served as a tomb: even the most spacious were so choked up that it was scarcely possible, in passing them, to find a place of rest for the foot, except in putting it on a corpse. Before the doors of the churches this miserable spectacle was in its fullest extent of horror. The sufferers, finding a sort of melancholy consolation in breathing their last sad sigh on a spot they regarded as holy, thronged around these edifices, and lay there heaped together, in a manner the bare idea of which chills and revolts the soul. . . .

A task even more painful to the survivors than that of succouring the afflicted during the malady, was that of disembarrassing the house of the dead body when any one expired. The more a friend has been dear during his life, the more does the heart revolt from the sight of that friend deformed and degraded by the stroke of death. If, then, the idea of approaching a corpse be at all times sufficiently revolting, how much greater must be the repugnance to approach one infected with a contagious malady! It was vain to expect that any motives, either of charity or interest, could induce a stranger to relieve the relations from this melancholy care; so that the latter, after having kept the corpse perhaps two or three days, was obliged at last, spite of the repugnance of nature, to submit to so painful a duty. The child performed the obsequies of his parents, the parents of their children. Some carried, some dragged the body out of the house; and those who were unable to do the one or the other threw it out of the window. Some of these corpses where wholly naked; others wrapped in an old sheet, blanket, or other rag—some were in their usual clothes—these were usually such as had died the most suddenly, after a few hours' illness. Some were rolled up in their mattresses, and others tied to a plank which had served as a bier to carry them, and a very, very small number were in coffins.

Among this mass of dead were an infinite number of children of all ages; for the physicians observed, that they always had the disease with the greatest violence, so that very few escaped. Some of these bodies were seated resting against the doors of houses, and in all kinds of attitudes, remaining in those in which the stroke of death had found them, and in general so hideous and deformed in all their features, that they were no longer to be known. This fatal disease makes impressions which remain even when the body has become clay; and as if it were not content to destroy life, but exercized alike its fury after death, the remains corrupt sooner in those who die of this malady than of any other, so that in ten or twelve hours the corpse exhales an odour altogether insupportable. What must the infection then have been after this evil had continued for some days! —Some of the bodies were half decayed, and so corrupted that the flesh dissolved as it were by the waters of the kennels, ran with them down the stream, and formed rivulets of putridity in the streets. We have seen the most beautiful woman in all Marseilles mingled indiscriminately with the other corpses in one of the squares. How many ministers of the Most High, alas! shared the same fate!

A spectacle even more horrible than all presented itself from time to time, and compelled the passenger to turn away from the spot, and seek another way to arrive at his destination. This was of miserable victims whom the phrensy of the disease had urged to throw themselves out of the window. One had his skull fractured, and the brains scattered all about—another streamed with blood from the wounds he had received—another had all his limbs broken. A further circumstance of horror was, that the dogs, starved by the desertion or death of their masters, ran about the city, and seizing on the bodies, dragged them about and devoured them. . . .

The vapours arising from the number of bodies thus left to corrupt in the streets infected the air, and spread the contagion to parts which had hitherto escaped. Some monasteries, as well as many private houses, which by being strictly shut up, and avoiding all intercourse with the town, had hitherto escaped infection, now began to feel the effects of these empoisoned exhalations. The moment seemed arrived when it was impossible that any one should be spared by the contagion; and when Marseilles, delivered over an entire prey to desolation, should not find one inhabitant remaining alive to tell her mournful tale to posterity. But it was even at this moment that the anger of Heaven, not willing that every soul should perish in a city which, from its flourishing state, he might be supposed to have viewed once with an eye of particular regard—at this moment he stretched out the arm of mercy towards her, and inspired those charged with the government with the means of remedy we shall here after explain. . . .

Nor was it the bodies alone which choked up the streets and rendered them impassable; they were equally obstructed by the quantity of wearing apparel, furniture, and other infected objects thrown from the windows of the houses, so that in many places clothes, mattresses, etc. heaped together and covered with mud, formed a barrier impossible to be passed. If the infection occasioned by this practice was infinitely dangerous, the only method taken to remove these objects was not without sufficient cause of alarm. Every day bonfires were made of them, as a general idea was circulated, that it was impossible to purge them of the contagion but by such a conflagration. In time, however, this prejudice was removed, or the town had been left totally destitute of these necessaries.

Such was the state of the city at the most dreadful epoch of the disorder. This continued till very near the end of September. . . .

The calm which had appeared towards the end of October was not of long duration . . . In effect, after All-Saints, many new sick appeared in different quarters of the city; above all in that of St. Ferreol, which had been the last attacked. But if the patients are new, the malady is uniformly the same; it presents the same character, the same symptoms, the same kind of malignity, though in a less violent degree, since many more in proportion of those who fell sick during the month of October recovered, than in the former periods.

The number of sick was also greatly diminished, the hospitals were now reduced to two, and of those who remained in the houses, not more than seven or eight fell sick in a week. The hospital of the convalescents, vacated entirely by the death of the majority of the patients, and the cure of the rest, was now abandoned: in the hospital of La Charité, 512 patients were received during the month of October, and only 181 in November. In the former month, 275 died, in the latter, 172; and in the same month, 94 were discharged cured. In October none were discharged cured, since it requires from thirty to forty days to perfect the cure; and it will be recollected, that this hospital was not opened till the beginning of October. In the hospital of the Jeu-de-mail, 357 sick from the city and territory were received during the month of October; and in November, 274. Of the former, 190 died, of the latter, 115. . . .

The convicts, meanwhile, continued to inter the dead, to transport the sick to the hospitals, to serve in the hospitals, and to keep the streets clean. An additional supply of 142 was given during the course of the month of October; and these, with the few that remained of the former supplies, served during all the remaining time of the contagion. On the whole, the number of convicts given for the service of the city amounted to 691. To these she is greatly indebted for her ultimate deliverance from this terrible calamity; and how much soever these unfortunate wretches may be in general esteemed the outcasts of human nature, the services they rendered us were not the less important, nor ought we, therefore, to feel the less grateful for them. Let us here adore that Providence, who thus ordained us a new subject of humiliation, in the necessity to which we were reduced of employing for the most important of all services, the most vile and despicable class of beings that the city contains within her bosom. Nor let us forget to confess our obligations to that illustrious prince, who had the goodness to afford us a succour so essential, or to those who executed his orders with so much wisdom and zeal.

Two causes concurred about this time to increase again the number of the sick. The malady being still in its utmost violence in the country, many of those whose peasants were sick, or whose families were attacked, fled from their bastides, and took refuge in the city, where the seeds of the disease which they had brought with them broke out. The commandant perceiving this, and, negligent of nothing which interested the public safety, issued new orders for the prevention of this abuse, and strictly forbade all entrance into the city, except to those who could produce a certificate from the officers of health, that no one had been sick in their bastide for the last forty days. Those who came daily to the city, such as the peasants who brought their commodities for sale, were obliged to renew their certificates every week. These regulations soon put a stop to this dangerous communication between the city and country, and the malady resumed its former progress of declension.

The avidity to take possession of an unexpected inheritance was also to many the fatal cause of their own destruction. Called to the entire succession of the wealth of a whole family, to whom, perhaps, they were very distantly related, and impatient to know the extent of their new acquisitions, they entered without precaution into infected houses, and, searching indiscriminately among the effects of the deceased, they often found what they sought not, and paid with their lives the forfeit of their cupidity. Their fatal heritage then devolved to relations yet more remote, fortunate if they could profit by such an example, and not fall equally martyrs to indecent and unreasonable transports. It was not, however, always the legitimate heirs on whom the punishment of their avidity fell; it was often those who found in the effects they stole the just forfeit of their crime. In vain had the commandant absolutely prohibited the removal of any clothes or effects from one house to another—a blind and headstrong rapacity, despised alike these wise ordonnances and the perils of the contagion. But in proportion as the times became more tranquil, and more attention could be given to minor objects, these orders were executed with greater severity.

Another abuse of a very singular nature occasioned, more than all, this partial renewal of the malady. Will it be believed? Scarcely had the contagion begun somewhat to diminish in its ravages, than the people, impatient to repair the mortality it had occasioned, thought of nothing but repeopling the city by new marriages—like mariners who have been in imminent peril of shipwreck, but are no sooner arrived in port, than, forgetting the danger they have escaped, they seek in new pleasures to drown the recollection of past troubles.[1] Our temples, long shut up, were now only opened for the administration of this sacrament. A species of phrensy seemed to have seized on both sexes, which led them to conclude the affair of all others the most important in the world, in the space of twenty-four hours, and to consummate it almost at the same instant. Widows, whose cheeks were even yet moistened with the tears they had shed over a dead husband, consoled themselves in the arms of a living one, who perhaps was in like manner snatched from them a few days after, and in a few days more they were wedded to a third. In short, such was the passion which had taken possession of the people, that if the usual time of gestation could have been shortened, we should soon have found the city as populous as before the malady. Let us leave to the physicians, by whom it was started, the discussion of the question, whether this frantic passion was or was not a consequence of the malady, while we seek to account for these marriages on grounds more sensible and reasonable.

An infinite number of artisans and persons of all sorts and situations were left without wives, without families, without relations, without neighbors. Returning to their accustomed occupations, and not being able to spare the time necessary to arrange the affairs of their houses themselves, or provide for their own sustenance, they knew not what to do single, and found themselves under the necessity of marrying again immediately. Others, whom the poverty and misery of their situations had precluded before this calamity from all idea of marrying, now on a sudden become rich, either by the immense gains they had acquired in serving the sick, or in transporting the dead,— by the unexpected inheritance of a property from which they were very far removed, or by means more easy and concise than any of the

[1] Modern demographers have often noticed this tendency on the part of eighteenth century men and women. The tone of moral reprobation adopted by Bertrand is out of place, for this desire to get on with the business of living was very largely responsible for recouping demographic losses inflicted by epidemic disease. See André Armengaud, *Démographie et Sociétés* (Paris, 1965).

above,—now for the first time in their lives finding themselves in a situation to gratify this universal and most natural inclination of every human being, it was not surprising that they should hasten to enter into a connection which had so long been the object of their eager wishes. To these may be added a number of girls of all ages, who, left desolate in the world, and no less embarrassed with the state in which they found themselves, than with the fortunes to which they were become heirs by the death of all their relations, thought there was no better resource than to throw themselves into the arms of a husband. Above all, those who, from some deformity of person, had been precluded all hopes of marriage, and had no other prospect than a convent for their portion, found themselves too happy in the change that had taken place in their views not to be eager to enter the first moment possible into the state for which they sighed. And it often happened, amongst a numerous family, that if one was more ugly or deformed than the rest, it was she who escaped the disease; while the eminently beautiful fell its first victims. Young men whom the fear of a father had prevented from contracting marriages, perhaps, little suitable to their situation, now freed from this constraint, hastened to satisfy a blind passion with which they had been long possessed, and to dissipate a fortune they had no hopes of enjoying so soon. Such were the motives which influenced the greater part of these marriages;—the effect of them was to banish from among the people that sadness and consternation which the terror of the contagion had spread among them. It was then, that houses in which a few days before nothing was heard but sighs and groans, resounded with cries of joy, and that the utmost sadness and desolation was succeeded by sports and festivities,—shall I say it?—by the ball and the dance. Strange blindness! which, in rendering us insensible to so many misfortunes, might draw upon us yet greater in future!

But so many marriages hastily concluded and consummated, were the occasion of spreading anew the fatal infection. It often happened that, while one party was totally free from the malady, the other yet but imperfectly cured, and bearing about in his body the lurking principle of the disease, communicated it to his wholesome partner, who dearly paid the rashness of which he had been guilty. To prevent these abuses, which could not fail to protract the evil, it was agreed between my lord bishop and the commandant, that no license of marriage should be given, unless the parties demanding it could produce certificates of health from the physicians. The abatement of the sickness gave the latter gentlemen leisure to attend to this point:—

in effect, it now became for some time their principal occupation to receive the disagreeable visits of those who were frantic to rush into the bonds of marriage.

If the people had shown no other signs of having forgotten their past misfortunes than the joy which these new marriages occasioned, there would have been no reason to fear that a ceremony honoured by the first miracle of our Saviour, authorized by the laws, and necessary to society, could irritate the Lord anew against us, provided all was conducted in conformity with Christian decency and rectitude. But what was very likely to draw down upon us yet greater judgments from his anger, were the thefts, the plunderings, and an infinity of other crimes now perpetrated, the horrors of which we dare not here retrace. For these their perpetrators promised themselves impunity on the part of men from the troubles of the contagion, and absolution on the part of Heaven by the favour he had shown them, either in their having escaped the disease entirely, or recovered from it, when it proved mortal to so many thousands of their fellow-citizens. While the arm of the Lord was yet extended over us, a general license was seen to reign among the people, a depravity of morals frightful to think on. Some seized on houses left vacant by the mortality; others forced open those which were shut up, or only guarded by persons incapable of resistance. They entered those where, perhaps, there remained only one person languishing with the malady, forced open the closets and drawers, and took away whatever they found most precious, often carrying their infamy even to the length of delivering themselves from an importunate witness, who had otherwise but a few moments to live. These enormous crimes, much more frequent in the height of the malady than in its decline, were generally committed either by those who served the sick, who carried away the dead, or who attended at the hospitals. By the declarations which these people from their situations were enabled to wring from the dying, they were informed of the state of their houses; nay, it often happened even, that by the same means they got possession of their keys. . . .

This license was yet greater in the country, where the distance of the bastides[2] from each other, and the opportunity of going to them in the night, favoured these criminal expeditions. It will easily be supposed, that in the end these stolen clothes and effects must spread the infection, and occasion fresh attacks of the malady.

Disorders thus flagrant could not be of long continuance under a

---

[2] *Bastide* is the Southern French word for a country cottage.

commandant whose strict rectitude and firmness of character kept the whole city in awe. As it is under favour of darkness that villains are bold in committing crimes, he made an ordonnance which forbade people unknown to go about the city as soon as night began, and to persons known after the retreat was sounded at nine o'clock, and even till that hour they were not permitted to go out without a torch. He caused all public places, public-houses, and houses of pleasure, so pernicious to innocence, to be shut up. The patrols were observed more strictly, and the rounds were made more regularly; the strictest search was made in the city and country for all suspected persons, and the prisons were soon filled with these malefactors. Many deposits of infected clothes were discovered as well in the city as in the country;— all those women whose occupation it is to corrupt youth were seized and confined; while frequent executions repressed the licentiousness of the people, and finally put a stop to crimes, capable of drawing down upon us still greater judgments from Heaven.

The criminals were judged by the chamber of police. This tribunal, at which the commandant himself presided, was become sovereign, and judged finally during the time of the contagion. . . . Many persons were condemned by it to death, to the galleys, and to other punishments, and all civil affairs were also referred to its jurisdiction. Before this tribunal many young students of the law pleaded, and, in these early efforts, gave promising assurance of what might be expected from their maturity. It was for a while almost overpowered with the multiplicity of affairs; and above all, by proving odd and singular inheritances to which the death of so many persons intestate and that of entire families gave rise.

4   FROM   *Abbé C. Chevalier (ed.)*
Tableau de la Province de la Touraine, 1762–1766

Population growth brought its own difficulties, of which the primary one was the pressure on the land to produce more food. Given the technical level of the age, the difficulties of transportation, and the customary methods of cultivation, land holding

SOURCE. Abbé C. Chevalier, ed., *Tableau de la Province de la Touraine, 1762–1766* (Tours: Imprimerie Ladeveze, 1863), pp. 254–255. Translated for this volume by Susan Kaplow.

and servitude imposed both by the landlords and the village community, this could be a very difficult goal to attain. Starvation was now a less frequent occurence than it had once been, but the peasant's lot was far from easy, and peasants comprised four-fifths of the population.

The report on the generality of Tours, a relatively rich part of Western France, shows that prosperity was not impossible. The creation of new markets for grain through export benefited small-holding peasants as well as larger proprietors. But in most instances when agricultural prices went up, it was because of shortage, and shortage generally meant that the small proprietors had little surplus to send to market once the needs of their families had been met. Similarly, the landless day laborer was likely to be a victim of a price increase despite the fact that he worked the land. This was because commodity prices quickly outran any rise in wages.

In the Auvergne, a habitually underprivileged region in which peasants were constantly subject to the loss of their livelihood, only the annual migration of a good part of the male population made existence possible. The yearly trek to the city was a necessity; the proceeds were meager, especially in terms of the work and discomfort involved. Taxes took what little the migrants managed to save; disease and debility did the rest. Those who survived, if we are to believe Chevalier, were infected by the evil habits of city life and forever rendered inapt for the simple joys of the villages. Here we have the reiteration of the town versus country conflict that is the dark side of eighteenth century urban development, arising directly out of the real threat posed to the maintenance of the village community.

The report from the Sarthe describes the situation on the eve of the Revolution. It might be—and was—duplicated a thousand times in as many areas. Beggary was so common an occurrence in the countryside that few thought of it as anything but perfectly normal, not in the least morally wrong or contemptible. But that it was too often "the apprenticeship of crime" is also beyond doubt.

The report from which these notes are drawn is believed to have been written by a certain de Voglie, chief engineer of the generality of Tours.

The continual increase in food prices during these three years [1764–1766] ... can only be attributed to the freedom to export grain which, having become generalized in 1764, gave grains a value that they could not otherwise have had because of the impossibility of marketing them and because of the lack of buyers. Wheat and other grains suitable for feeding human beings being the product most necessary to their existence, the price of other foodstuffs must indisputably be based on their value [i.e., the value of grains], in proportion to the greater or lesser utility of each. ... By facilitating the exportation of grains, the increase in prices which has taken place was necessarily to be expected; it is certain that it is a real boon to landed proprietors. With the exception of this resource, agriculture was tending toward ruin, since it was useless to seek to increase production although keeping it impossible to market the goods. But it is nonetheless true that the benefits secured by exportation profit proprietors more than they do that part of the people who exist only by their work. In truth, salaries for all kinds of labor have increased, but the rise in prices had absorbed this increase. Their situation is therefore the same as it was before freedom of exportation; they have gained only the certainty that they will not lack for work, on account of the greater need proprietors will have for their labor in the culture of the soil and for the manifold objects of luxury. As a natural result of this increase, the profit of the proprietor must diminish little by little, since there is a limit beyond which it cannot go. The state alone will make a definite profit through the work it gives to the farmer, the advantage to it in increasing exports, and through the infinite resources of a greater circulation of coin. Its [the state's] object must be perfectly fulfilled, if it takes care, with wisdom and in full knowledge of what it is doing, to fix a limit to the freedom of exportation which will secure its subjects the quantity of grains not merely necessary to allow them to subsist but sufficient to prevent any forced increase in the habitual price of bread, either through overanxious hoarding or through lack of provisions in case of a famine year.

5   FROM   *Statement of the Causes and Effects of*
Emigration in the Several Parts of Auvergne Province
and on the State of the People

The authorship of this statement is unknown. It was written in 1787.

It is certain that the annual or total emigration is greater in the mountains than in the valley [Limagne], but the causes are very

SOURCE. "Apperçu des Causes et des Effets de l'émigration dans les différentes parties de la province d'auvergne et de l'état du peuple," in Archives Départementales du Puy-de-Dôme, 4 C 33. Translated for this volume by Susan Kaplow.

different in the two regions and, indeed, vary in the several parts of the mountains. The easiness of finding a better life has always been the motive that leads men far from the place that has nourished their childhood years.

In the low mountains to the east all the rye having been sown in the month of September, and the women sufficing to take care of the cattle, most of the men leave and scatter through the kingdom with a pick or a saw to seek work, because the nature of their land and the hardness of the climate leave them nothing to do and because they need money to pay their taxes, which the produce of their land does not completely supply.

This land produces grain, but everything else is lacking. And even the sale of this produce is uncertain due to the variability of the harvest, which is reduced considerably by too much drought or too much rain. The sale of young cattle, which the inhabitants pursue with all possible industriousness, is the only sure source of income. And as it is insufficient to pay the taxes, they supplement it by annual emigration. They go to work a part of the forests throughout France, to do road work or to work in the carrying trade. After that, they go to do the harvest work in Languedoc and Burgundy and then return home for their own harvest, and to replant the land that their wives have cultivated during the good season.

Thus it is that with the greatest sobriety and the most arduous work these men bring back each year the money necessary to pay the taxes of their district and even of the valley, to which they go to exchange part of the money earned outside the province for wine, hemp, iron and other goods that they don't have at home and which the valley furnishes them either from its soil or through its trade.

Those who have the most intelligence or are accustomed to the work, hire others and make a profit from their labor. These entrepreneurs have some money left over each year after they have paid their taxes.

Because they have little property, they buy up one after another the fields cultivated by their families or others that are within their reach. When they get to a certain age they are no longer in a position to make long trips and to sustain the arduous work of the forests and marshes. They retire to the domain that they have built up, believing that they may now enjoy the comfort they have acquired through thirty or forty years of forced labor. It is then that their misery begins, for they are obliged to deprive themselves of everything and to live more economically than ever in order to be able to pay the taxes with their own produce. They hope for better times and borrow from those who have replaced them in migratory labor. Their children pay off their debts by abandoning some part of their fortune to money lenders. Soon they contract new ones for the same reasons and the grand-children of him who had made his fortune hire out and return to the same work gangs that the grandfathers had organized, complaining that their fathers have ruined them.

He who is born with less intelligence or with less control over his senses always remains a worker . . . and never has anything but a small salary. What he brings back is absorbed by taxes and when age forces him to stay home his misery is as frightful as was that of his wife and children during his absence. It is increased still further if nature has given him daughters instead of sons, who would have been able to help him with the proceeds of their labor.

One often sees these individuals wandering about the district, happy just to make a living. During the cold season they don't even stop working to take a meal, for fear of getting cold and not being able to continue their day's work and earn the sum necessary to buy bread. During the winter of 1766, one of the worst of the century in Auvergne, a troop of people were working in a wood a quarter of a league from Fredeville. They dug a hollow to live in, so as to save the time that would have been needed to go and come from the village. They spent the whole winter this way. One froze to death.

This picture shows to what extent emigration is necessary in all these districts and how villages pay more in taxes than their soil can produce. It is astonishing that this emigration is not total, and that need and the sight of misery does not destroy among the people the feeling that ties men to the place of their birth.

Beyond Langeac and toward St. Flour, the situation is still worse. The pastures cared for with much labor provide for a large quantity of young animals. The soil can usually furnish grain and wool for export. Men migrate only to be watercarriers or porters in Paris. They bring back greediness, sloth and all the other vices of big cities. With few exceptions, they ought never to migrate but ought to work harder.

The mountain range to the west of the province . . . is called the high mountains. Its produce is totally different from that of the low moun-tains. Its volcanic soil does not lack for nutritive elements, but the roughness of the climate at this elevation allows it to be used only as meadow or pasture land for the fattening of meat animals, of young stock and for dairy farming. . . .

The idleness and the little work demanded to care for livestock in winter has caused the men of this area to migrate to milder climates for work and better food. The canton of Besse supplies Paris with watercarriers and also boat haulers on the Loire.

Those who live in the environs of the mountains of the Cézalier go to the northern provinces of France to sell at retail merchandise that they carry on their backs. They are what are called packmen.

For a long time the inhabitants of the Cantal region have been engaged in the boilermaker's trade. The boiler factory established in Aurillac favors them in this kind of industry, which takes them even beyond the frontiers of the kingdom. The greatest number return each year and bring to the tax collectors and to their families the money they have earned. At last, repelled by these long trips, accustomed to an easier life and disgusted with agriculture, they take their whole family and move to the place where they have spent their winters, either abandoning their land or giving it away at the lowest price.

The need they have to find considerable money and the success they obtain in their travels attract them to such an extent that there are villages where not a single able-bodied man remains during the winter. Some take their children with them or rent them to others to do six months' work as chimney sweeps.

If, through constant sobriety, forced labor, and the most astonishing industriousness, they have succeeded in accumulating a few small sums before death catches up with them, their children go into the cattle trade. The product of this trade is less uncertain than that of agriculture and it depends on the industriousness of the person engaged in it. It can only employ those who have some capital to begin with.

It is these districts especially that need to be freed from the salt tax. The habit they are in of giving salt to their livestock almost every day must be added to the great amount they use in the manufacture of their cheeses, so that one can imagine how much harm is done them by the slightest rise in the price of salt. The area around the Cantal has been afflicted with a new misfortune in recent years, the need or perhaps even the desire to make greater profits has led many inhabitants to give up the boilermaker's trade to become pedlars for the most part. Most of them do poorly and do not return for several years. At last their unfortunate families learn that it is necessary to abandon the land that the creditors are going to have sold and from which they will recover only one half of their debt. These heads of families stay away a few more years without making an appearance, for fear of being arrested. So they leave their wives and small children and perhaps even their invalid fathers without resources and deprived of their support.

The big cities they have necessarily frequented have corrupted their morals, and they no longer feel the charms of a blameless rustic life. They return to and remain in the cities to flee taxes and to consume, all alone, the product of their work and industriousness.

The Limagne is the place where indigence is greatest. The inhabitants do not even have the cruel resource of seeking a living for their families elsewhere for part of the year, because the vines demand constant care. They cannot neglect them for one year without harming the harvests of following years. Some travellers who have crossed both the mountains and the valley have been struck by the external differences they see. In the mountains, especially to the west and south of the province, men are big and strong, their bearing and their confident air depict a well developed character and seem to indicate that they know that there is no real difference between one man and another. In the Limagne, on the contrary, they are small, ugly, bent and present only the image of men ground down by slavery, threatened by the least illness that may happen to them to be forced to have recourse to beggary, pursued without respite by need. They seem even to be ignorant of their superiority over the animals. The observer cannot recover from his astonishment when he sees all the signs of poverty surround him in a country that is so pleasing to the eye on account of its varied forms and of the wealth that nature has lavished there . . . He sees people live on bread made of rye mixed with barley whose bran has not even been removed. It is without any doubt the worst bread eaten in France . . . Never does the peasant go to the butchershop, and he eats a few pieces of salted pork four or five times a year only. He sells good grain and green beans he has raised in order to live on black beans which are used elsewhere only as fodder for livestock.

He sells his wine and throws water on the residue of his vat to make his best drink. If nature has given him several daughters, he employs them to gather in grass in the grain fields and limits his ambition to having a cow so as to cut down his work by coupling it to the plow together with his neighbor's cow. The butter he gets from it is sold and his soup and his vegetables are seasoned only with the same walnut oil that feeds his lamp at night.

The meadows and the smallest gullies are bounded by poplars and willows, the pruning of which every four years supplies the props needed for the vines.

The sides of the roads are planted with walnut trees, the harvest of which is so useful to the people, but unfortunately too often destroyed by the violent frosts of the winter or the late frosts of the month of April. If cold and frost kill off some of these trees they are sold to the rich who can find no other kind of wood for their fires, while the people in general build fires only with the leaves they gather in the autumn or the stems of thistles which grow in the poorly cultivated hillocks and fields of some rich people. The bread baking ovens are heated in general only with straw.

If the traveller pays attention to the peasants' dress, he is astonished by its coarseness. Except for the hat, he wears nothing that is not made at home. His suit is woven with hemp, and the white and black wool of his lambs, the mixture of which avoids the cost of dyeing the cloth. His leg, covered with the same material, shows his unstockinged bare foot in his wooden shoe. His neck is covered only by the cloth of his shirt. The tie worn among the people in almost all provinces is not used in Auvergne except by those propertyless persons who work other people's land, because it is a manufactured item for which money is needed, and the cultivator has no money. The public prints have sometimes depicted the surprise felt by travellers at the sight of a peasant's dwelling in Auvergne. Inside, nothing more comforting is found. On all sides one sees the peasant subject to all sorts of privations. Is it astonishing that these individuals give way to the excesses of wine, which have become so common? This is their only recourse in sadness, and their cheer on extraordinary occasions.

In some districts of this very fertile country, except near the cities, one can hire workers for eight sous a day, total salary without food. Every village contains many beggars. And while the mountain districts take eighteen months to pay one year's taxes, in the Limagne whatever may be the harshness of the tax collector, he often takes twenty four months to collect.

The high price that wine sometimes reaches seduces the peasant into planting this kind of crop. He enjoys two or three good years, and dies of hunger for six because the price happens to fall and he cannot cover his costs, while taxes remain the same.[1] This is the cause of the great misery of the people in wine country, and the misery is greater or lesser in each village according to the proportion of its area devoted to vines. If wine had a constant value, vine growing would be

---

[1] On the difficulties of the wine trade, see C. E. Labrousse, *Esquisse du movement des prix et des revenus en France au XVIIIe siècle* (Paris, 1933, 2 volumes).

very advantageous to the Limagne through its exportation to the mountains or sometimes even to Paris, but customs are a great barrier to securing the latter market.

Wheat is another export item for the Limagne, but it has found no market for a number of years and the storehouses of the rich are full. But they are not able to convert the grain into money.

One last thing will finish off the picture of the people's misery in this magnificent garden.

Several people have seen in various places, among others in the plain of Sauvetat, a woman harnessed beside a donkey, while her husband guides the plow.

This is in order to do a hurried work more quickly, for in no other region are so few cattle used in working the fields and so much land worked with the spade. No district of France is cultivated with as much economy, for one sees almost no hillocks, and no hedge occupies a place that can produce grain. The roads are as narrow as possible . . . and enclosure walls are very rare . . .

There is a middle term between the mountainous area and the Limagne . . . often designated as the half mountain. There one sees the bare rock, the foot of the mountains is buried in the plain. Their summits are covered with grass or grain, but the slopes of their ridges are too precipitous and have been stripped [of their topsoil] by the rains and are a horrible sight. The inhabitants of these districts are the poorest of the Limagne. Their wine is of the worse quality and always sells less and later than other wine. Their taxes are fixed at a time when their hillsides had recently been cleared and were still productive. The province, and they above all, still bare this burden, although the terrain has become absolutely useless. There is not a single landlord who has not experienced a loss of landed revenue through the abandonment of certain plots. And what remains in cultivation is more open than elsewhere to drought and to the harm caused by the rains and so often disappoints the expectations of the harvesters and forces them to have recourse to emigration. As they have fewer vines than their neighbors in the Limagne, they can absent themselves, but only for three to four months a year. These are the districts that provide chimney sweeps to a part of France, watercarriers to Paris and the workers in the ocean ports. Often they stay away several years at a time, or do not come back at all. Then the loss of manpower becomes noticeable, because the vine culture demands many hands. So it is that the same region supplies migrants in winter but lacks for hands in summer.

Here, as in the mountains, the tax collector takes all the money that
has been brought back from abroad. It is neither libertinage nor the
desire to run away that makes people leave, but need. A village that
saw sixty of its inhabitants take up residence in other provinces
between 1767 and 1781 has lost only two or three people since 1781,
because every winter since that time a public works gang has been
organized and is open to everyone who wishes to take part. Freedom
from the salt tax and its reputation for fertility, along with other causes,
have led to overburdening this province with taxes. Need has forced
the inhabitants to have recourse to emigration . . . but this emigration
becomes a great evil for those districts whose inhabitants do not
return. In all parts of the province one sees villages that are totally
destroyed. The wealthy proprietor can find almost no domestic
workers or tenants for his farms in the low mountains and none at all
in the high mountains.

The inhabitants of the cantons of Langeac and Paulhaguet ought
never to migrate. If some means were found to get the peasants of the
half mountains work in the winter, they would give up their travels.
Their still pure morals tie them to their homes, whereas corruption
has made great progress these last few years in the high mountains.
May the beneficent administration created by the sovereign for the
happiness of the people reestablish the spirit of competition and
sobriety in the countryside, and an increase in the trade of the prod-
ucts of the soil.

Caillard d'Allières

6   FROM   *Mémoire sur la Mendicité Déposé au
Bureau du District de Mamers*

Those whom the law must protect and not punish, those whom
humanity and the public interest compel us to aid today form a
group which is unfortunately too large. It is these people whom we
have called the worthy poor. They become so because they lack a daily
occupation or because their salaries are not in accord with the price of
provisions. Or because bad weather, sickness, infirmity and age have
diminished or completely taken away from them that work whose

SOURCE. "Mémoire sur la mendicité déposé au bureau du district de Mamers par
M. Caillard d'Allières, président. . . . March, 1789," in Archives Départementales
de la Sarthe, C 94. Translated for this volume by Susan Kaplow.

price alone assures their sustenance and that of their families. In all such cases, these people must be given the necessary supplement [to their incomes]. For it is commonly recognized that they should not have to come to ask for it from those who have the means and a humane spirit.

Having a great number of children also leads to beggary. To prove this, one has only to compare the modest expenditure of a man and his wife to the sum which a man who works solely with his hands makes. The year consists of 365 days and 10 sous a day is the minimum necessary for the food of a man and a woman living together in a small household; this makes 182 livres. The least rent for a cottage must be 20 livres, and it cannot cost the two people less than 40 livres to take care of their clothing, undergarments, shoes, tools, etc. Thus a sum of 242 livres, 10 sous is necessary for the maintenance of two people living together. The working year has only 295 days since there are 70 holidays and sundays. Another 30 or 35 days should be deducted for snow, rain and frost, which interrupt outside work. One can therefore reasonably calculate only 260 working days. The common daily wage in this region for laborers and for many artisans is 12 sous, and 5 sous for women. This makes 17 sous which, multiplied by 260, only amounts to 220 livres. The more strenuous work of the month of August can add another 24 livres, making a total of 245 livres.

But Oh! Providence! Their parsimoney enables them to raise in their own home and without outside aid their first child. But others [may be] born, or illness, lack of work or a greater wasting of time may occur. In all these cases, they must either be helped at home according to their real needs, or they must be allowed to keep the right to ask charitable people for their help. But as the number of needy people grows larger daily and charity, however extensive, cannot suffice, they are almost forced to become bandits and thieves.

Beggary is the apprenticeship of crime. It starts by making one love idleness, which everywhere will always be the greatest moral and political evil. In such a state, the beggar, without principles, or at least without the habit of honesty does not long resist the temptation to steal. Soon nothing further restrains him in his projects of rapine but fear of punishments visited on lawbreakers. And as soon as he becomes sufficiently adept to persuade himself that he will always escape the pursuit of the police, he at the least steals every day and often becomes a professional robber. Among brigands there are very few who did not become so through this most terrible progression, whose first step is beggary and whose prime cause is indigence.

II THE NOBILITY

The French nobility had been living in a state of more or less constant crisis since the sixteenth century. After their decimation in the religious wars, the appearance in France of new or absolute monarchy tended to strengthen the state apparatus at the expense of the nobility. Although neither Richelieu nor Mazarin wished to destroy the nobles, they hoped to subordinate them to the monarchy in order to put an end to any pretentions they might have to the exercise of independent power. No longer were nobles to play the principal military and administrative roles, which had permitted them to keep the monarchy in a dependent postion. The tables were now turned, and it was made clear to the unhappy nobles that their only road to preferment was through loyal service to the crown. This policy was carried to its zenith under Louis XIV, who even went so far as to choose certain of his ministers among men of humble (or at any rate, common) origin. The Sun King gave his nobles bread and circuses in the form of the inflated ritual of court life at Versailles, but he refused to allow them effective initiative *as a class* in shaping state policy. For instance, he deprived the parliaments of their part in the legislative process by taking from them the right to issue remonstrances against royal edicts.

The nobles raged at their impotence but often became lost in the petty considerations of pride and precedence, in the manner of the Duc de Saint Simon in his celebrated *Mémoires*. By so doing they made the royal system of subordination legitimate. There was no longer any argument about the equity of the court hierarchy, but only about the place one should occupy in it.

After the death of Louis XIV in 1715, the initiative for a restoration of noble authority came from the nobles of the robe, the magistrates of the sovereign Courts of Parliament. Many of them were new men, in the sense that their families had been bourgeois two centuries or less before. They cared more for the exercise of power than for the dry dust of genealogical history. The first move was to restore the right of the parliaments to remonstrate, and this was accomplished by reaching an agreement with the Duc d'Orléans, whereby the will of Louis XIV was broken and he was appointed regent with the full approval of the magistrates. The monarchy would have cause to regret this agreement many times in the course of the century.

Under the leadership of the robe, the entire nobility closed ranks and reasserted its claim to political and economic power. Its economic power, sometimes weakened and varying from place to place and family to family, had never really been destroyed. A modified form of seigneurial control was still very much in existence, although serfdom had been abolished almost everywhere. In the years between 1715 and 1789 there ensued a series of attempts to make the land yield greater amounts of revenue. This has been called the seigneurial reaction, but it may be variously interpreted. In some ways, it meant the introduction of modern techniques of land holding and exploitation; in others, the squeezing of the peasant in the grip of an archaic system of village agriculture, by the application and enforcement of the letter of seigneurial law, not to mention the exercise of pressures unknown to feudal lawyers. This movement was full of contradictions, but in sum it may be seen as an attempt to modernize French agriculture within the framework of seigneurial institutions for the benefit of the privileged landowner.

Concerning political power, the French nobility insisted on pursuing an independant course so that there was constant friction between itself and the monarchy. Although we may doubt that a common front between them would have forestalled the Revolution, there can be no denying that, as Tocqueville noted, the split in their ranks made it easier for the revolutionary movement to secure its first victories.

The politics of the nobility required a certain ideological justification. Why should the nobility play the role to which it so clearly aspired? The answer to this question is found in the argument from fundamental laws so often brought up by the robe magistrates, and of which the Bordeaux remonstrance of 1771 against Maupeou's dissolution of the parliaments is an excellent example. The argument had the posthumous blessing of so eminent a figure as Montesquieu, who had himself been a magistrate in that city's parliament. In recognizing monarchical authority the nation had reserved certain rights to itself, rights that were not conferred by the king but had grown out of immemorial usage—most important, the right to participate in the making of the laws. The parliaments exercised this right in the name of the Nation, as long as a larger (more representative?) assembly was not called into existence. Monarchy implies law that binds even the monarch; a king's failure to obey the law leads to despotism.

The right of the parliaments to exercise legislative power was upheld by the nobility, because the magistrates (nobles of the robe) were members of the Second Estate. The existence of such intermediary bodies was a guarantee against the abuse of monarchical authority. More fundamental, however, was the concept of nobility itself. Why was there a nobility at all? The most common answer to this question in the eighteenth century was an appeal to history to the effect that nobility derived from the Franks who had conquered the Gallo-Romans in the fifth century. Henri, comte de Boulainvilliers (1658–1722) gave this argument its first literary expression in his *Essais sur la Noblesse de France*, of which excerpts are reprinted here. It should be noted that the theory presents certain major difficulties. First, its assumptions are racist. This did not make it morally or scientifically unacceptable to the eighteenth century, but it did create the necessity of identifying the members of the master race. Unfortunately, it was impossible to do so. Second, by insisting on the idea of noble blood ("true and incommunicable nobility") Boulainvilliers created divisions within the nobility that were likely to get in the way of united action. For him, the men who migrated into the nobility with the connivance of the monarchy were more of a threat than the bourgeoisie and the people, an attitude that was to be expected of a man who called the feudal system "the masterpiece of the human spirit." Although the argument from fundamental law was supposed to justify the *de facto* power of a ruling class, the argument from the right of conquest was intended to defend the exclusive power of an ancient nobility (that had all but ceased to exist) within the framework of feudal institutions. Boulainvilliers was hopelessly out of touch with eighteenth century realities, and his theory, more than any other, deserves to be seen as the last gasp of a dying order.

Now, not all nobles were rich and powerful. There were many who languished in provincial obscurity, eking out a meager living but intensely proud of their origins and status. In fact, it would be only a small exaggeration to say that pride (and, hence, attachment to the old way of doing things) was inversely proportional to wealth and power. For every noble who gamboled about Versailles and Paris, there were dozens who tended their quiet gardens and wished for nothing more than to go on doing so in the accustomed manner. The Revolution did not come to France as punishment for a corrupt nobility. Despite the sermonizing on this point of certain contemporaries like the Marquise de La Tour du Pin, France was not a sink of corruption in the tradition of Ancient Rome. The Revolution found a good part of the nobility backward and unable to allow for change, but these are not moral considerations. The account of his childhood in a Breton chateau by the great romantic writer François-René de Chateaubriand (1767–1848) will, I hope, give some idea of the atmosphere that reigned among the provincial nobility, of which the isolation, the meanness and the discipline of life at Combourg were by no means atypical.

7 FROM *Très-Humbles et très-Respectueuses Remonstrances qu'Addressent au Roi, Notre très-Honoré et Souverain Seigneur, les Gens Tenant sa Cour de Parlement à Bordeaux*

This is one of a series of protests against the dissolution of the Parliament of Paris by Maupeou in 1771. The parlements were attacked by the enemies for having an "esprit de système" that sought to trouble public order. The following is a reply from the Bordeaux Parliament.

Our system, Sire, (your Courts of Parliament have never known any other) was and always will be to cause justice to reign, to see to the happiness of the population, to the observation of the laws and to keep intact the sacred depository confided to us and to punish anyone who dares to violate it.

Our principles exist with the monarchy, monarchy cannot exist without them.

Before subjugating the Gauls, the Franks had laws or rather tacit agreements under which they had formed an association, and which usage had consecrated. We find these laws and customs [still in use] after the conquest of the Gauls; they form the constitution of the French monarchy. They assure the nation the rights to assist in the formation of new laws.

We find, under the first race of our kings, several references to the Assemblies of the Champ de Mars,[1] which prove the assistance [given] by the nation.

SOURCE. *Très-Humbles et très-respectueuses remonstrances qu'adressent au Roi, notre très-honoré et souverain seigneur, les gens tenant sa cour de Parlement à Bordeaux* (Bordeaux, 1771), pp. 7–9, 11–12, 15–16, 20–23, 27–28, 30–31. Translated for this volume by Susan Kaplow.

[1] The Champ de Mars refers to the meetings held by the Franks before and after their conquest of Gaul. Nineteenth century and earlier historians looked upon these assemblies as the beginnings of representative government, but modern research has shown that this belief has no basis in fact.

The kings of the second race maintained the right of the nation to assist in the exercise of legislative power. . . .

[Charles the Bald] recognized that the orders of kings could only be considered to be laws in so far as the French had accepted them and ordered that they be observed. . . .

The terrible mixture of anarchy and tyranny created by feudal government and the strange ignorance into which all the orders of the state fell for several centuries caused all the laws to go unobserved. For a long time, no public power was known in the realm; the rights of the prince and of the nation were indeterminate. Nevertheless, one sees the parliament assembled several times in this era of disorder and confusion; and its right to assist in framing legislation is almost the only one of the fundamental laws to survive this chaos.

Thus, from the foundation of the monarchy to the reign of Philip the Fair, the nation was maintained in its right to assist in passing legislation: there is no law without its consent. . . . Even if your Courts of parliament, Sire, hadn't the right to examine and verify such new laws as it may please your majesty to propose, this right could not be lost to the nation. It is imprescriptible and inalienable. To attack this principle is to betray not only the nation but kings themselves; it is to overthrow the constitution of the kingdom, to destroy the foundation of the monarch's authority. Can it be believed that verification of new laws in the Courts of parliament does not fulfil this original right of the nation? Could public order profit from its being exercised once again by the nation? As soon as your Majesty deigns to reestablish the nation in the enjoyment of its rights, we shall no longer demand the sort of authority which your royal predecessors have granted us.

But until then, Sire, be so kind as to consider that the verification of new laws is a duty inseparable from our functions: there is no law without verification, as there could be none without the consent of the nation assembled.

Is this rule of state merely an empty formula? Has the population been told of an examination, a verification of the laws to which they are to be subject only as a means of fooling them more surely, by forcing your Courts of Parliament to register them without examination or against their conscience? Do entries of laws on the court registers carried out by order of the king suffice to give the king's will the sanction and character of law? Would it then be possible to order the magistrates to approve, by their silence or their presence, the infringement of fundamental laws? Could they fail to speak the truth without betraying the state and the sovereign? Could they be forced to fool the population themselves, by allowing it to believe that they have verified and registered [an edict] when there has been neither examination nor deliberation?

A long time ago it was said in your name and presence "that the Courts of parliament were the depositories of the sacred rights of the crown and of the liberties of the realm; that the king had confided this portion of his authority to them". They were ordered to use it with the steadfastness that their consciences demanded.

In the very first moments of your reign you recognized, Sire, that you could do nothing more advantageous for your service than to reestablish the ancient freedom of verification of parliament. Oh! how could the laws be verified without this freedom? Verification necessarily supposes examination and deliberation, and there can be no deliberation without freedom of choice.

We will not hide from you the fact, Sire, that this freedom has been infringed more than once; but the protests of your Courts of Parliament have always maintained the fundamental law of free verification. The numerous efforts of arbitrary power have always failed or, at least, its temporary successes have served only to prove the wisdom and utility of the established way of doing things; these very successes have strengthened the dominion of the fundamental law.

Such is the dominion of the fundamental law in your realm, Sire, that it sustains and perpetuated itself by its own strength. The greatest, wisest and best kings, the very ones who were most jealous of their authority, have not hesitated to recognize this fact. The more attacks have been made against the fundamental law, the more it has been proven that it is bound to the monarchy and can perish only with the monarchy.

Your Courts of parliament, Sire, have always used the freedom the fundamental law gives them for the welfare of the state and the glory of the king. If they have resisted [your orders] it was to defend your rights or those of your predecessors; and never have they shown more zeal and fidelity than when they seemed to oppose the will of those who held the reins of state.

[The king's evil advisors] do not wish to recognize any of the fundamental principles of the monarchy. The new law presented on your behalf [to destroy the authority of parliament] excludes them all. It establishes a law that destroys all laws. It is desired that your Parliament sitting in Paris should receive and have executed, as laws, all the wishes that will seem to emanate from Your Majesty, even when just

motives keep them from proceeding freely to their registration. Remonstrances are permitted, and they may be reiterated. But to order
at the same time that, in case of a perservering royal will, the transcrip-
tion of the edicts on the registers of your courts, done in your presence
or by bearers of your orders, replace and have the same effect as a free
and thoughtful verification—is this not to destroy the apparent freedom we have to speak to you of the needs of your people? Is this not
to render vain and fruitless our right to make you hear their groaning?
And, finally, it is not, under the guise of the specious mildness of
monarchical government, really to exercise the rigors of despotism?

8 FROM *Henri, Comte de Boulainvilliers*
Essais sur la Noblesse de France

It is certain that in common law all men are equal. Violence has
introduced the distinctions of freedom and slavery, of nobility and
commoners; but although its origins be vicious, this usage has been
established for so long a time in this world that it has acquired the
force of a natural law.

The first monarchies of the East, the Medes, the Babylonians and the
Persians, were founded on the dignity of the nobility, whose task it was
to govern the inferior peoples under the authority of the Sovereign.
It is to this union between the nobles and the prince that one must attribute the long duration of these first dominions. On the contrary,
peoples amongst whom the ambition of individual persons has not
been subordinated to a superior body, which ties together and unites
the diverse members of a State under the authority of a chief common
to them all, have always been subject to continuous revolutions. . . .

It is therefore true that men are all naturally equal in the share they
have of reason and humanity. If something distinguishes individuals
one from the other on a personal basis, it ought to be virtue or the
proper use of that reason; but it would be incorrect to conclude from
this principle that it is the only distinction that ought to exist among
men.

SOURCE. Henri, Comte de Boulainvilliers, *Essais sur la Noblesse de France* (Amsterdam,
1732), pp. 1–2, 7–10, 17–19, 224–230, 251–252, 298–300. Translated for this volume
by Susan Kaplow.

The examples of early times [Greece, Rome] that we have just touched upon make known to us the antiquity, use and necessity of nobility; the perils and disorders of a State, when nobility ceases to occupy the first place in it; and that same reason which makes us understand what is owed to virtue, makes us feel that virtue is more often found among good races than in others. One must also agree that virtue needs the *éclat* of fortune to make itself known, and fortune is usually conferred by birth, or a certain fatality that is not always attached to real merit. Noble birth is therefore the most common means of showing off virtue and causing it to be honored.

All the efforts of those who ironically make use of the Satires of Juvenal and Boileau against the nobility can prove only two things: either that a man without sense and without righteousness is unworthy of the nobility, or that a truly generous noble ought to imitate his ancestors and walk like them in the ways of honor and virtue; but these two truths are beyond all contest. Just as it would be absurd to base oneself on one's nobility then to plunge into luxury and debauchery and to authorize violence and injustice, so it would be unreasonable to make an argument of the praise of virtue against the nobility, which professes to it [as a principle]. Speak out as you will against those whose lives are a shame for the nobility; but do not claim, under color of this invective, to use the arms of your jealousy against that very nobility which is born of virtue, and which virtuous men have always respected since its first appearance on the scene.

Let the great actions of a warrior, the prudence, equity and virtues of a magistrate or a minister raise him, if one wishes, above the ancient nobility; this distinction is a personal one and is passed on to his children only on condition that they be as virtuous and as fortunate as he; for it is just that those who should always have the privilege of rank be those whose long line of ancestors, illustrious through their marriages and the services they rendered to the Motherland, have gained the title of a true and ancient nobility: a title that creates a right that is absolutely not for sale in the marketplace, which the favor of princes can neither give nor communicate with riches and employments, since it is attached to the blood that gives us birth. . . .

The Franks were originally a people of the North, foreigners in regard to the Gauls and the Romans and consequently counted amongst the Barbarians, whose impolite and boorish mores merited the name well enough; but above all their hatred for the name, language and customs of the Romans. For the rest, they were lovers of liberty, valiant, light headed, disloyal, avid for wealth, unsettled, impatient. So it is that ancient authors describe them. Freedom for them did not consist of exemption from the fatigue of war, since, on the contrary, even women wanted to take part in it; but freedom lay in the exemption from any sort of tribute and in the maintenance of their customs. That is why they never wanted to submit to the Romans, nor receive the territories offered them, preferring to conquer a dwelling place at the point of their swords than to renounce their laws and customs to embrace those which reigned in the Roman Empire. They considered the right to choose their captains and kings as the surest means to avoid oppression, and they obeyed them only in war. In peacetime, kings and captains kept their authority only in proportion to their exploits: they had no greater part in public deliberations than private persons, if they had not merited the confidence of the people by their actions or if they had not greater eloquence than the others to convince them of their points of view.

[*Boulainvilliers argues that all Franks were freemen, but that there had been a nobility among them prior to the invasions of the Roman Empire. They conquered the Gauls and ruled over them. All Franks participated in making decisions. They established kings in order to defend their liberty. The Gauls became subjects not of the king, but of the nation as the owners of the land.*]

These privileges . . . were in use . . . ever since the time when the Franks had lived beyond the Rhine. But after they had conquered Gaul, they acquired three others, which remained attached to the blood of the conquerors: that is, to the French Nation. But they never claimed to owe these privileges to the liberality or favor of princes; as indeed they depended on neither one nor the other. The first of these privileges was the general exemption from the onerous burdens of the state, except for military service at the proper age. The second was authority over the people of Gaul, with a formal distinction such as between master and slave. The third was the power to possess in usufruct and in parts their newly conquered lands and domains, according to the rules that had been adopted. . . .

[*The true nobility, Boulainvilliers continues, has declined as a result of the increase of royal power. From the fifteenth century onwards, a combination of court intrigues, foreign corruptions (like the regencies of Marie de Médicis and Anne of Austria) and the high cost of living at court has ruined the nobility.*]

The best blood of the realm perished in the Wars of Religion, or by the efforts of ministerial ambition, or sees itself reduced to obscurity and poverty by the exactions of the tax farmers. Finally, ever since that time, history no longer shows anything but an extreme confusion of all the members of the state: the great estates have passed into the hands of favorites, money into those of private individuals, usurers, men of the robe, while the nobility, ruined and scorned, is reduced to a small number of families who scarcely remember their ancient grandeur.

Thus it can be said that the good old days of the nobility have passed, because it was too poor [an economic] manager and not careful enough about the glory of its predecessors when the hope of present fortune caused it to embrace the phantoms of the court and of favor, and to forget its own dignity.

We are sharing the destiny of Ancient Rome, where all the first families died out or were relegated to obscurity, when the form of government was changed; but we also must recognize that this is a destiny common to all states of long duration. The world is a plaything of continual change. Why should the Nobility, with its possessions and advantages, not be subject to the common rule? One must be neither irritated nor jealous at the elevation of those obscure families who have taken over the work of our fathers, and who have come to enjoy the glory they left to their Motherland. It will perhaps come to pass— and for my part I hope so—that some one of our children will cut through that obscurity in which we live to recover for our name its ancient *éclat*, and then we will no longer complain of the vicissitudes that will raise us up after having cast us down.

But to return to our subject: it is necessary to admit that in proportion to its taking up duties in the court, so did the Nobility loose its natural *éclat*. One becomes accustomed, in imitation of princes, to put more value on their favors than on one's own qualities. The interested obedience practiced there [at court], adulation, intrigues that lead to fortune, tie those who succeed rather to an accidental grandeur, whose creators they take themselves to be, than to the grandeur they might enjoy from their birth. Formerly the nobility, faithfully attached to the person of the king by the religion of their oath, honored and cherished by him as the bulwark of the crown, shone alone in the important posts, not fearing that favor might do it harm, nor that its inferiors might replace it. The number and newness of its competitors today excites its jealousy, as the multitude of jobs foments its ambition, and these two attractions have ruined its property and consequently sapped its hopes at the base. . . .

It is the need of money that has led the nobility to forget itself to such an extent, that it is no longer ashamed to mix its blood with that of the lowest commoners, nor to pass it into its own veins. The daughters of the rich tax farmers are avidly sought out, because that is the only way to buy big offices, or to pay debts that service or luxury at the court have caused old families to contract. And thus it is not a rare thing to see in positions of power the children of those whom our fathers called public thieves. . . .

But if our century so often witnesses the effects of private ambition, it sees no less commonly the fall of these fortunes built without the solid foundation of a true nobility. One cannot consider without astonishment the present state of the families of those who in our own time have occupied a ministry with more authority and wealth than our ancient kings had. They will soon crawl like the others and will abase themselves more and more, when the alliances that support them cease to give them protection. . . .

Let us say then that in the confusion to which we are exposed by so many changes in mores, in men's minds, in war and in government, it is not astonishing that we have forgotten what old nobility is; or, if we still remember, we strive to abolish its rights, even by inducing the royal authority to do so; as if, in truth, its grandeur [i.e., the grandeur of the monarchy] depended on a poorly regulated mixture of the blood of all its subjects, such as takes place among the Turks. New families, not content with the equality they have attained, claim preference over old ones by virtue of their employments and riches which assure them all the dignities they can buy; and finally by virtue of the favor they think they possess, or to which they aspire. But despite all that, if (misfortune of the century!) the needs of the state favor their ambition for a certain time, these same causes will despoil them in a little while and will plunge them once again into the obscurity from which they came.

True and incommunicable nobility always remains and cannot fail to reassert itself with distinction under princes as learned and as equitable as ours, when the luster of birth is upheld by true merit.

9   FROM   *René de Chateaubriand*
                    Mémoires d'Outre Tombe

I was born a gentleman.[1] In my view, I have profited from the chance
of my birth by maintaining that firm love of liberty which rests prin-
cipally with the aristocracy, whose last hour has come. The aristocracy
has three successive ages: the age of superiority, the age of privilege,
the age of vanity. Once past the first, it degenerates in the second, and
dies out in the last. . . .

Three branches constituted the line of the Chateaubriand family,
of which two were financially ruined. The third, that of the lords of
Beaufort, continued in a branch (the Chateaubriands de la Guer-
rande), grew poorer through the inevitable effect of the country's
law.

Following Breton practice, the eldest sons took away two-thirds of
the property; the younger ones divided among themselves a single
third of the paternal inheritance. The decomposition of their already
paltry stock ensued the more rapidly as they got married.

Since this same distribution of two-thirds to one-third was also
valid for their children, these younger sons of younger sons quickly
came to the sharing out of a pigeon, a rabbit, a duck pond and
a hunting dog. For all this, they were still *high knight and powerful
lords* of a dove-cot, a frog pond, and a rabbit warren.

In ancient noble families, one sees many younger sons. One
follows them for two or three generations; then they disappear,
having slowly fallen to the level of peasants or been absorbed into
the working classes, and one cannot find out what has become of
them. . . .

The impoverished Breton nobility had one last recourse: the royal
navy. Of this they tried to take advantage for my father. But he would
have had to go to Brest, live there, pay his teachers, buy a uniform,
arms, books, mathematical instruments. How could all these expenses
be met? The commission sollicited from the minister of the navy failed
to arrive, because there was no patron to request its dispatch. The
chatelaine of Villeneuve fell ill with grief.

SOURCE. René de Chateaubriand, *Mémoires d'Outre Tombe* (Paris: Librairie Garnier
Frères, no date). I, pp. 15–16, 21–22, 24–25, 72–74, 108–116. Translated for this volume
by Susan Kaplow.

[1] I.e., a noble.

It was then that my father showed the first sign of that resolute disposition which I knew in him. He was about fifteen. Having seen his mother's anxiety, he approached the bed where she lay and said to her: "I no longer wish to be a burden to you."

When she heard this, my grandmother began to cry (I have heard my father describe this scene twenty times). "René," she answered, "What can you do? Cultivate your plot of land."

—But it cannot feed us; let me leave.

—Alright, said the mother, Go where God wishes you to.

Sobbing, she embraced the child. That very evening my father left his mother's farm and arrived in Dinan, where one of our relatives gave him a letter of introduction to someone in Saint-Malo. The orphaned adventurer embarked as a volunteer on an armed schooner which set sail several days later.

At that time, the small republic of Saint-Malo alone upheld the honor of the French flag on the seas. The schooner joined the fleet which cardinal Fleury had sent to aid Stanislas, beseiged by the Russians at Danzig.

My father landed and was engaged in the memorable battle in which fifteen hundred Frenchmen, commanded by the brave Breton de Brehan, count of Plélo, gave on the 29th of May, 1734, to forty thousand Moscovites led by Munich. De Brehan, diplomat, warrior, and poet, was killed, and my father was twice wounded.

He returned to France and reembarked. Shipwrecked on the coast of Spain, he was attacked and stripped of everything by robbers in Galicia. He got passage on a ship at Bayonne and turned up at home. His courage and spirit of order had won him a name. He emigrated to the Islands, grew rich in the colony, and laid the foundations for the new fortune of his family. . . .

I used to spend my vacations at Combourg. Chateau life in the environs of Paris is nothing like chateau life in a distant province.

The property of Combourg consisted in all of heaths, some windmills, and two forests, Bourgouet and Tanoern, in a region where wood is almost without value.

But Combourg was rich in feudal rights of different kinds. Some represented fixed payment for certain concessions, or established practices originating in the old political order. Other seem to have stemmed from amusements.

My father had reactivated several of these latter rights in order to avoid their prescription. When all the family was together, we took part in these gothic diversions. The three principal ones were the *Saut des Poissoniers*, the *Quintaine*, and a fair called the *Angevine*.

Peasants in wooden shoes and old-fashioned trousers, men of a France which is no more, watched these games of a France that was no more. There was a prize for the winner and a forfeiture for the loser.

The *Quintaine* preserved the tournament tradition; it probably had some relation to the old military service given by the fiefs. It is very well described in du Cange. . . . One had to pay fines in ancient copper coins up to the value of [50 sous].

The fair known as the *Angevine* took place yearly in the prairie of the Pond, on the fourth of September, which was my birthday. The vassals were obliged to take arms; they came to the chateau to raise the banner of the lord. From there they went to the fair to keep order and lend force to the collection of a tax due the counts of Combourg for each head of cattle. This was a sort of amusement tax.

At this time of year, my father kept open house. We danced for three days: the masters in the great hall to the scraping of a violin; the vassals in the *Cour Verte* to the nasal tune of a bag-pipe.

There was singing, shouting, and shooting of rifles. These sounds blended with the lowings of the stock of the fair. The crowd wandered through the gardens and the woods and, at least once a year, something resembling joy could be seen at Combourg.

Thus, I have been rather oddly placed in life to have been at the meets of the *Quintaine* and the proclamation of the Rights of Man; to have seen the bourgeois militia of a Breton village and the French national guard; the banner of the lords of Combourg and the flag of the revolution. I am almost the last witness of feudal customs. . . .

Entrenched in his manor, my father never left it even when the Estates[2] were meeting. Every year my mother spent six weeks in Saint-Malo at Easter time. She waited for this as for a deliverance, since she detested Combourg.

A month before the journey, they spoke about it like some perilous undertaking; they prepared for it; they let the horses rest. The evening before it, they went to sleep at seven o'clock and got up at two in the

---

[2] The Provincial Estates of Brittany, an organization dominated by the extremely numerous Breton nobility, was staunch in the defense of its prerogatives against monarchical infringements.

morning. To her great joy, my mother left at three and took the whole day to go twelve leagues. . . .

I would enjoy recalling the customs of my parents even if they were only a touching memory to me. But I will evoke the picture even more willingly as it will seem to be a tracing of scenes from a medieval manuscript. Between the present time[3] and the time which I am going to describe there are centuries.

When I returned from Brest, four masters (my father, mother, sister and myself) inhabited the chateau of Combourg. The only servants were a cook, a chambermaid, two lackeys, and a coachman. A hunting dog and two old mares were sheltered in a corner of the stables. These twelve living beings disappeared in a manor in which one would scarcely have noticed a hundred horsemen, their ladies, their squires, their valets, the steeds and hounds of King Dagobert.

In the entire course of the year, no outsider came to the chateau, except for several gentlemen, the marquis de Montlouet, the count de Goyon-Beaufort, who asked for hospitality on their way to plead in the parliament. They arrived in winter, on horseback, pistols in their holders, hunting knives at their sides, followed by a valet also on horseback carrying a large livery holder behind him.

Always very ceremonious, my father received them bare-headed on the porch in the midst of rain and wind. Once inside, the countrymen spoke of their wars of Hanover, their family affairs, and their legal cases.

In the evening, they were taken to the north tower, to the apartment of *Queen Christine*. This was the room of honor, which held a bed seven feet long in every direction, with a double curtain of green gauze and crimson silk, held up by four gilded cupids.

The next morning, when I came down to the great hall and looked through the window at the flooded and frost-covered countryside, I saw only two or three travelers on the solitary road by the pond. These were our guests riding toward Rennes.

These outsiders were not knowledgeable about life. Still, through them, our view was extended by several leagues beyond the horizon of our woods. As soon as they had left, we were reduced, on weekdays, to a family tête-à-tête and on Sundays to the company of the village bourgeois and the neighboring gentlemen.

Sundays when the weather was good my mother, Lucile and I went to church by crossing the little *Mail* along a country road. When it

[3] Chateaubriand was writing during the July Monarchy.

rained, we followed the abominable rue de Combourg. Unlike the abbé de Marolles, we were not driven in a light carriage drawn by four white horses taken from the Turks in Hungary.

My father only went to the parish church once a year at Easter. The rest of the year he heard mass in the chapel of the chateau. Seated in the seigneur's pew, we received the incense and the prayers facing the black marble sepulcre of Renée de Rohan adjoining the altar. Image of the honors of man: a few grains of incense before a coffin.

The distraction of Sunday ended with the day; they were not even regular ones. During the bad weather, whole months went by without a single human creature's knocking at the door of our fortress.

If the sadness was great on the heaths of Combourg, it was even more so in the chateau. Under its vaults one felt the same sensation as in the monastery of Grenoble. When I visited this last in 1805, I crossed a desert which was ever increasing. I thought it would stop at the monastery. But I was shown, within the very walls of the cloister, the gardens of the Carthusians, which were even more abandoned than the woods. Finally, in the center of the monument, enveloped in the folds of all this solitude, the old cemetery of the monks a sanctuary from which eternal silence, the god of this place, spread his power over the surrounding mountains and forests.

The dismal calm of the chateau de Combourg was heightened by the taciturn and unsociable disposition of my father. Instead of drawing his family and his servants closely around him, he had dispersed them to the four winds of the building.

His bedroom was placed in the small east tower and his study in the small west tower. The furnishings of his study consisted of three black leather chairs and a table covered with deeds and parchments. A family tree covered the mantle and in the embrasure of one window were all kinds of arms. . . .

My mother's room was above the great hall between the two small towers. It had a wooden floor and was decorated with cut Venetian glass. My sister had a room adjoining my mother's. The chambermaid slept far away up amongst the large towers.

As for me, I was ensconced in a sort of isolated cell, at the top of the turret of the stairway which led from the inside court to the different parts of the chateau. At the foot of this staircase my father's valet and servant lay in the vaulted cellar and the cook was garrisoned in the wide west tower.

Summer and winter, my father arose at four in the morning. He used to come into the inside court to wake up his valet and call him to the foot of the turret stairway. . . . He was brought a little coffee at five o'clock and then worked in his study until noon.

My mother and sister breakfasted in their rooms at eight. I had no fixed times for getting up or eating breakfast; I was supposed to study until noon: most of the time I did nothing.

At eleven-thirty, they rang the bell for dinner, which was served at noon. The great hall was at once dining room and living room and we dined or supped at its eastern end. After the meal, we moved to the western end by an enormous fireplace. The great hall was decorated in wood painted greyish white and bedecked with old portraits from the reign of François I to that of Louis XIV. Among these portraits were once a Condé and Turenne. Above the fireplace hung a painting depicting Hector killed by Achilles under the walls of Troy.

Dinner over, we stayed together until two o'clock. Then, in summer my father went fishing, went out to his vegetable gardens, walked a short distance. In fall and winter, he went hunting and my mother retired to the chapel, where she spent several hours in prayer.

This chapel was a somber oratorium, hung with good paintings by the greatest masters, the kind of paintings one would not expect to find in a feudal chateau deep in Brittany. Today I have a painting on copper of the holy family by de l'Albane: this is all that remains to me of Combourg.

With my father gone and my mother at prayer, Lucile retired to her room and I went back to my monk's cell or went running through the fields.

At eight, the bell announced supper. After supper, in good weather we sat on the porch. Armed with his rifle, my father shot at the wood-owls who came out of the crenels at nightfall. My mother, Lucile, and I looked at the sky, the woods, the last rays of the sun, the first stars. At ten o'clock we went inside to bed.

Autumn and evening winters were of a different kind. When supper was over and its four participants had returned from the table to the fireplace, my mother would throw herself down with a sigh on an old day bed of worn Siamese print. Near her stood a candle in its holder.

I sat down near the fire with Lucile. The servants cleaned up and left the room. My father began his walk, which would not stop until bed-time. He was dressed in a gown of curly white wool, or rather a a kind of coat which I have only seen on him. Half-bald, his head was covered with a large white bonnet which stood straight up. During his walk, when he moved away from the hearth, the huge room would be so scarcely lit by its single candle that he could no longer be seen.

We would only hear him as he walked in the shadows. Then the light slowly returned and he emerged little by little from the darkness, like a ghost in his white robe, his white bonnet, his face long and pale.

Lucile and I spoke a few whispered words while he was at the other end of the room; we fell silent when he came near. Passing us, he used to say, "What were you talking about?" Seized with terror, we would not reply; he would continue walking. The rest of the evening, the only sounds were the measured ring of his footsteps, my mother's sighs, and the murmuring of the wind.

Ten o'clock sounded on the chateau clock: my father stopped. The same spring which had raised the clock's hammer seemed to have suspended his footsteps. He would pull out his watch, wind it, take a large silver torch with a candle atop it, enter for a moment the small west tower, then come back, his torch in hand, and go toward his bedroom off the small east tower.

Lucile and I used to wait for him; we kissed him and wished him goodnight. He leaned toward us his dry and hollow cheek without a response, continued on his way and retired to the furthermost end of the tower; we heard its doors close after him.

The charm was broken. My mother, my sister, and I, transformed into statues by my father's presence, would come back to life. The first result of our disenchantment was an overflowing of words: If silence had oppressed us, it paid for it dearly.

When this torrent of words had flown forth, I called the chambermaid and showed my mother and sister to their rooms. Before I could retire, they made me look under the beds, in the fireplaces, behind the doors; inspect the stairways, and the adjoining passages and corridors.

They remembered all the traditions of the chateau, robbers and ghosts. People were sure that a certain count of Combourg with a wooden leg and dead these three centuries, appeared at certain seasons and had been encountered in the big stairway of the turret. His wooden leg was also supposed sometimes to walk about with a black cat.

The whole time of my mother's and sister's preparations for bed was taken up with these stories: they got into bed dying of fear. I retired to the top of my turret; the cook went back into the wide tower; and the servants descended into their cellar.

My tower window looked out on the inside courtyard. During the day, I could see the crenels of the wall opposite, where vines crept and a wild plum tree grew. Some swifts who, in the summer, plunged into the wall's holes with a cry, were my only companions.

At night, I could see only a small piece of sky and a few stars. If the moon was shining and setting in the west, I knew it only because of the rays which came through the diamond-shaped panes of the window. Wood-owls, flying about from one tower to the next, passing again and again between the moon and me, cast on my curtains the moving shadow of their wings.

Relegated to the most deserted place, at the entrance to the galleries, I missed not a murmur of the shadows. Sometimes, the wind seemed to run fleet-footedly; sometimes it heaved plaintive sighs. Suddenly, my door would be flung open, the cellars would bellow, then these sounds would die out, only to begin again later.

At four in the morning, the voice of the master of the chateau, summoning his valet to the entrance of the age-old vaults, rang out like the voice of the last phantom of the night. . . .

The stubbornness with which the count de Chateaubriand made a child sleep alone in the top of a tower could have had bad effects; but it was advantageous to me. This violent way of treating me gave me a man's courage without depriving me of that faculty of imagination which people today want to take away from youth. Instead of trying to convince me that there were no ghosts, they forced me to face up to them.

When my father would say to me with an ironic smile, "Is *monsieur le chevalier* by any chance afraid?" it was as if he had made me sleep with a corpse.

When my excellent mother would say to me, "My child, nothing happens except if God wills it; you have nothing to fear from the evil spirits if you are a good Christian," I was more reassured than by any philosophical reasoning.

I became so inured that the night winds in my uninhabited tower served only as toys for my caprices and wings for my dreams. Once kindled, my imagination spread to every object, nowhere found sufficient food for itself, and would have devoured heaven and earth. . . .

III THE BOURGEOISIE

The role of the bourgeoisie in the preparation of the French Revolution has been the subject of heated debate among historians for some years now, especially since the end of World War II. Before that there seems to have been general agreement that the bourgeoisie, however defined, had indeed made the Revolution and profited from it through the introduction of a capitalist socioeconomic system in France. But how was the bourgeoisie to be defined? Was it a heterogeneous collection of non-nobles or a class of capitalist entrepreneurs, a bunch of vociferous lawyers, or a group of republican conspirators? For lack of an answer, everyone continued to talk about the bourgeoisie, each man giving the concept the content he found concenial. More recently, however, it has been seen that this lack of rigor in definition is unacceptable, and that we must, therefore, find some means to connect the bourgeoisie to the realities of the eighteenth century or give up the concept altogether.

There are historians only too willing to cry out that the emperor has no clothes on, the emperor in this case being the Marxist school of historical analysis. It is my view that this is too hasty a conclusion. The Frenchmen whom we normally call bourgeois included in their ranks some capitalist entrepreneurs, but also lawyers, rentiers, land owners, and professional men of all descriptions. The practice of capitalism is not their common denominator. Clearly, the nineteenth century bourgeoisie did not yet exist in 1789. What is left? A group of non-noble (but not necessarily nonprivileged) persons whose occupations, life styles, aspirations and, latterly, consciousness placed them outside the norms established by a crisis-ridden but nonetheless still dominant nobility. Because as individuals they were refused access to prestige and power within the framework of old regime institutions, they came to define themselves as a class in whose interests it was to reshape those institutions.

The relationship of the eighteenth century bourgeoisie to the means of production may be stated this way: the expansion of economic activity and the creation of new (capitalist) forms of enterprise and wealth over a period of several centuries gave rise to (bourgeois) men and ideas that were outside the accepted patterns of behavior and thought sanctioned by the traditional ruling class. Capitalism created the bourgeoisie, but the two words are not synonymous, nor is the latter merely the agent of the former. They live in a symbiotic relationship shaping each other's development and that of society as a whole through the conflicts engendered between them and the traditional rulers. Not all bourgeois are capitalists, but they could not exist outside a developing capitalist system—at least not in the first instance.

Consciousness of patterns of social change or even of their own interests on the part of the bourgeoisie took a long time to mature in eighteenth century France, as contemporary foreign observers often noted. The publicist John Andrews (1736–1809) and Dr. John Moore (1729–1802) were both British and highly aware of the differences between their own country and France, particularly in regard to class relationships. They were quick to blame what they took to be the servility of the French bourgeois and were certain that they would be incapable of making a revolution to measure up, in terms of Whiggish liberty, to the English Revolution of 1688. They proved wrong, but their reports did not present a distorted picture of the situation. The lawyer Edmond-Jean-François Barbier (1689–1771), whose diary is one of our major sources for the history of Paris in the reign of Louis XV, corroborates them fully when he writes of the tendency of the bourgeois to ape the behavior of the nobility.

But consciousness was developing, slowly but surely. Some, like the Abbé de Véri, regarded the change of heart within the "middle layer of society" as unfortunate and looked back with nostalgia to their youth, when obedience and servility were the order of the day. On the other hand, men like Brissot and Clavière, both of whom were to become leading figures among the Girondins, exemplify the very movement the good Abbé deplored. In a single paragraph, they not only damn those who look upon commerce as an unworthy occupation but also raise doubts as to the legitimacy of aristocracy—the kind of attitude required to make a revolution possible. What was still wanting was a theoretical formulation of the same point of view— or at least one that would capture the imagination of a large number of people, while serving as a platform for the redistribution of social power. This was provided by Sieyès in his *Qu'est-ce que le tiers état*. It is a brilliant summation of the teachings of the philosophes. On the basis of a Lockean labor theory of value, Sieyès equates productivity with social utility and thus arrives at an impassioned defense of the Third Estate's contribution to the commonweal. The Third Estate *is* everything and therefore *has a right to* everything, not least of all political power. That power, separated *à la Montesquieu* and used in accordance with Rousseau's concept of popular sovereignty, together with the benevolent action of a free and competitive market, will guarantee the greatest happiness for the greatest number.

For the sake of comparison and to show how much ground had been convered in not much more than twenty years, I have also included a selection from the Abbé Jaubert's *Éloge de la Roture* [In Praise of Commoners] of 1766. Jaubert (1715–1780) was a priest and minor literary figure from Bordeaux. His polemic is a moral tract against the pretentions of the nobility, but nowhere does he propose to revolutionize society and to substitute a new set of rulers for the old. Aside from the fact that Jaubert is rather more of a traditional Christian than Sieyès, that is the major difference between them; there can be none greater.

To end this section, I have chosen selections from the memoirs of François-Yves Besnard (1752–1842), a bourgeois priest who spent most of his life in and around Angers in western France. I have tried to give the reader a feeling of life in the small- and medium-sized provincial towns toward the end of the old regime. At the same time, readings of this type show that a good part of the provincial bourgeoisie was rather conservative in its habits and more than willing to continue living in the accustomed way. It would be wrong to imagine the existence of a monolithic, united bourgeoisie in the old regime. Even the unity achieved in the struggle against the monarchy and nobility would be short-lived. Although the disintegration of the revolutionary coalition, even as between bourgeois, was due to very specific circumstances of the Revolution itself, their disagreements may be seen as rooted in the variety of roles they played and the life styles they enjoyed over the years before 1789.

10 FROM
John Moore
A View of Society and Manners in France, Switzerland and Germany

The philosophical idea, that Kings have been appointed for public conveniency; that they are accountable to their subjects for maladministration, or for continued acts of injustice and oppression; is a doctrine very opposite to the general prejudices of this nation. If any of their kings were to behave in such an imprudent and outrageous manner as to occasion a revolt, and if the insurgents actually get the better, I question if they would think of new-modelling the government, and limiting the power of the crown, as was done in Britain at the Revolution, so as to prevent the like abuses for the future. They never would think of going further, I imagine, than placing another prince of the Bourbon family on the throne, with the same power that his predecessor had, and then quietly lay down their arms, satisfied with his royal word or declaration to govern with more equity.

I have heard an Englishman enumerate the advantages of the British constitution to a circle of French Bourgeois, and explain to them in what manner the people of their rank of life were protected from the insolence of the courtiers and nobility; that the poorest shop-keeper, and lowest tradesman in England, could have immediate redress for any injury done him by the greatest nobleman in the kingdom.

Well, what impression do you think this declaration had upon the French auditory? You will naturally imagine they would admire such a constitution, and wish for the same in France:—not at all. They sympathized with the great; they seemed to feel for *their* want of importance. One observed, "C'est peu de chose d'être noble chez vous": and another, shaking his head, added, "Ce n'est pas naturel, tout cela."[1]

When mention was made that the king of Great Britain could not impose a tax by his own authority; that the consent of parliament,

SOURCE. John Moore, M.D., *A View of Society and Manners in France, Switzerland and Germany*, 2nd ed. (Paris: J. Smith, at the English Press, no date), I, pp. 36–37, 41–43.

[1] "What a small thing it is to be a noble in your country,"—"All that just isn't natural [i.e.,normal]."

particularly of the house of commons, was necessary, to which assembly people of their rank of life were admitted; they said with some degree of satisfaction, "Cependant, c'est assez beau, cela."[2] But when the English patriot, expecting their complete approbation, continued informing them, that the king himself had not the power to encroach upon the liberty of the meanest of his subjects; that if he or the minister did, damages were recoverable at a court of law, a loud and prolonged *diable* issued from every mouth! They forgot their own situation, and the security of the people, and turned to their natural bias of sympathy with the King, who they all seemed to think must be the most oppressed and injured of mankind.

One of them at last, addressing himself to the English politician, said, "Tout ce que je puis vous dire, Monsieur, c'est que votre pauvre Roi est bien à plaindre."[3]

This solicitude of theirs for the happiness and glory of royalty extends in some degrees to all crowned heads whatever: But with regard to their own Monarch, it seems the reigning and darling passion of their souls, which they carry with them to the grave.

11 FROM   *John Andrews*

A Comparative View of the French and English Nations in Their Manners, Politics and Literature

The French merchants are a very respectable and working class of men, no ways inferior to our own. They differ from them however in several instances; in working more than the prodigious hurry so many of them are in to exchange that sphere of life for, what may be called the hobby-horse of every Frenchman, the rank and privileges of a noble. . . . A Frenchman however is completely satisfied with such a bargain [giving money for a title]; which . . . frees a man from the vulgar appellation *bourgeois*, so hateful to the ears of a modern Frenchman. . . .

SOURCE. John Andrews, LL.D., *A Comparative View of the French and English Nations in their Manners, Politics and Literature* (London: Printed for T. Longman and G.G.J. and J. Robinson in Pater-Noster Row, 1785), pp. 149–151.

[2] "However, that is nice."

[3] "All I can say to you, Sir, is that your poor king is much to be pitied."

Bourgeois is a term of reproach, which every man is sure to hear, who is daring enough to enter the lists of altercation with anyone who thinks himself by birth or office secured against the retortion. And yet the meaning of it is no other, strictly speaking, than that of a burgess, or citizen. But whereas no man in this island of liberty deems himself disgraced by being so called, in France it is quite otherwise. One may always perceive a consciousness of inferiority in the tone and accent of those who acknowledge themselves members of that little reverenced fraternity.

. . . The word bourgeois in the mouth of a French gentleman is always intended as a stigma, and never understood but as an expression of contempt, unless in legal processes, political discussion, or formal translations, wherein it appears in its proper genuine signification of those classes of the community that are below the rank of nobles.

12 FROM   *E.J.F. Barbier*
Chronique de la Régence et du Règne de Louis XV ou
Journal Barbier

(February 1725)—Monsieur Dodun, comptroller general of finances and extremely rich, acquired the marquisate of Herbault, near Orléans, and the office of the King's lieutenant for Orléans. It seemed to him too bourgeois to remain a man of the robe, especially since he possessed the *cordon bleu* [the military decoration of the Order of the Holy Spirit].

He put on a sword, had himself called the marquis d'Herbault, and, among other things, decked himself out in a gold-braided uniform resembling nothing so much as that of a police officer. Since Mr. Dodun is greatly hated, people looked into his past and found that his grandfather had been a lackey. Last but not least, they made up songs about him and his wife which were sung by everyone including bootblacks. Because of this, Madame Dodun spent eight sleepless nights.

SOURCE. E.J.F. Barbier, *Chronique de la Régence et du Règne de Louis XV ou Journal de Barbier* (Paris: G. Charpentier et Cie., 1857), I, pp. 379–380; II, pp. 362–363. Translated for this volume by Susan Kaplow.

Here is one of the songs:

> Dodun to his tailor said,
> "I'm called marquis d'Herbault now,
> Since at last I'm so well bred,
> Dress me like a lord and here is how:
> Deck me out in braid
> For I'm a gentleman,
> Deck me out in braid,
> I'm the king's lieutenant.
>
> Said the tailor, "My good man
> I would anyone defy
> To look more like a noble than
> You, when I clothe you bye and bye.
> We'll deck you out in braid
> You're ancestor was a gentleman,
> We'll deck you out in braid
> He wore braid like you.
>
> Madame Dodun to her hairdresser ran,
> "A gorgeous hairdo I require,
> For I wish to, as I know I can,
> Tender feelings in men inspire.
> Cut my hair, curl it, and comb it,
> I'm as good as any duchess
> Cut my hair, curl it, comb it
> I'm dining at the palace.

(November 1732)—The twentieth of this month there was buried a certain Peirenc de Moras, forty-six years old, *maître des requêtes*,[4] and head of the council of madame the Dowager Duchess [of Orléans?]. This man was the son of a barber and wig-maker from a small town in the Saintonge; he himself had shaved people.

Then he had come to Paris, place of refuge for all kinds of persons, where he sold junk and conducted his business in the street before that infamous year of 1720. He was involved in more bad transactions than in good ones. But, since he had nothing to lose, he put all his money into the scheme and was lucky enough to make a profit.

---

[4] The *Maîtres des Requêtes* were venal officers who acted as judges and administrators in matters referred to them by the King's Council. Intendants and holders of other major offices were often recruited from their ranks. Thus, this office was considered a way station on the road to more prestigious public employments.

He had a flair for finding ways to get ahead in this country. So he died leaving twelve to fifteen million *livres* in real estate, furniture, jewels, and shares in the India Company. In the faubourg Saint-Germain he built for himself the most superb house in all of Paris.

He leaves a widow and three children. This widow is the daughter of Fargès, a former army supplier and originally a soldier. He had an income of five hundred thousand *livres* and possessed the secret of avoiding the payment of any of his debts. They say that, while still a nothing, Moras had charmed the daughter of Fargès and gotten her pregnant, thus obliging the father to give him his daughter. More than one lord at court is thinking of marrying this rich widow.

This alone shows the true colors of our government. Here is a nobody who in two years time has become richer than princes, and this fortune, produced by this unfortunate system, is made up of the losses endured by two hundred individuals on their family property or on property acquired after thirty years work in all sorts of occupations. But this man was allowed to keep his fortune, because he was in a position to distribute a million to lords and p[rostitutes] of the court; and he was given an honorable office in the magistracy!

13 FROM *Baron Jehan de Witte (ed.)*
Journal de l'Abbé de Véri

The following entries in the diary are dated 1776

The middle layer of society no longer has the veneration for royalty that our fathers had for its divine origin. Our minds are getting accustomed to looking at the sovereign only as the administrator of the nation. The blood of kings is a phrase devoid of meaning to many people. Hereditary succession no longer has anything but the common utility of the nation to support it. All this tends to move men away from that enthusiastic and servile submissiveness that provided earlier kings with the blind instruments of their despotism. The number of these instruments will decrease every year.

SOURCE. Baron Jehan de Witte, ed., *Journal de l'Abbé de Véri* (Paris: Jules Tallandier, no date), **II**, pp. 8, 18–19. Translated for this volume by Susan Kaplow.

. . . The monarchy ought not to ignore the fact that the military spirit of former times has disappeared and will return no more. In my youth I saw old soldiers on whom the word king made the same impression that the word God makes on the most religious hearts. This word justified everything and led them to do all sorts of things. It was sufficient for them to rush blindly into danger, with a kind of satisfaction.

Philosophical reflections on the equality of men, on the natural liberty of each individual, on the abuses of the monarchy and on the absurdity of religious veneration of a class of families, the example of the English colonies in America; books in everyone's hands and the spread of knowledge which gives rise to the weighing of everything on the scale of natural right, all this has given rise to ideas about monarchical religion and revealed religion in general that are very far from those that were dominant during my youth. The bold and decisive tone of conversations astonishes me when I recall the time when people almost distrusted their own brother or friend in these two matters.

According to the ideas of the present day, there is no question of removing one king in order to replace him with another. An absolute indifference reigns as to who may have a right to the crown, and there is a secret desire to the rid of any pretention to government by right of birth. The enthusiasm for the blood of our kings that I still saw in my youth no longer appears to be the spirit of the nation. So that I wouldn't be astonished if a bet I have heard proposed actually comes to pass, that there would no longer be a monarchy in France and in England in half a century.

14 FROM   *Brissot de Warville and Etienne Clavière*
Considerations on the Relative Situation
of France and the United States of America

In France, I say it with pain, the science of commerce is almost unknown, because its practice is dishonoured by prejudice; which

SOURCE. J. P. Brissot de Warville and Etienne Clavière, *Considerations on the Relative Situation of France and the United States of America* (London: Logographic Press for Robson and Clarke, 1788), p. xi.

prevents the gentry from thinking of it. This prejudice, which is improperly thought indestructible, because the nobility or gentry are improperly thought one of the necessary elements of a monarchical constitution; this would alone be capable of preventing French commerce from having activity, energy and dignity, were it not to be hoped, that sound philosophy, in destroying it insensibly would bring men to the great idea of estimating individuals by their talents, and not by their birth: without this idea there can be no great national commerce, but aristocratical men will abound; that is, men, incapable of conceiving any elevated view; and men contemptible, not in a state to produce them.

15 FROM *Abbé Jaubert*
Eloge de la Roture Dédié aux Roturiers

If the nobility thinks one of its most precious prerogatives to be that of being able to pride itself on an origin that is lost to the memory of man, what advantage ought not the commons to draw from their own, for, far from being ignorant of its source, they can trace it back to the first days of the creation of the universe.

Man was, in truth, the final work of the divinity, and he was the most perfect and most accomplished. God created him in his image, endowed him with a reasonable and immortal soul, gave him pre-eminence over all creatures, put him in a place of delights so that he might busy himself in conserving it; with one exception, God gave him permission to use all created beings and, as a sign of the authority given him over all the animals, God wished them to receive from him the names most proper to them.

So great a number of privileges accorded the first man was an evident sign that He who had created him looked upon him as his masterpiece, and that He was pleased to lavish upon him all his favors. But however scrupulous Holy Writ is not to forget any of the favors God showed to Adam, it does not tell us that he was created noble: on the contrary, it seems that the Bible seeks to insinuate in every sentence in which the matter is raised that he was created a commoner.

SOURCE. Abbé Jaubert, *Eloge de la Roture dédié aux Roturiers* (London and Paris: Chez Dessain Junior, 1766), pp. 11–13, 17–19, 24–28, 76–77, 80–82, 90–92. Translated for this volume by Susan Kaplow.

During all the time that the most beautiful ages of the world lasted, there was no sign that pride and vanity had introduced any rank of distinction among mortals: our forefathers, equal among themselves, recognized as superiors only those to whom they had pledged their faith by the hommage naturally due to the heads of families, so that domestic authority might cause order to reign. One finds the origin of the arts necessary to their survival, needs or comforts; but one does not know that men formed among themselves different classes and that they claimed to raise themselves, by virtue of their birth, above others who shared a common origin with them.

It cannot be said that Adam was created noble. If that were true his posterity would have inherited this advantage in the same way that they have succeeded to the punishment his disobedience merited. One must agree that he was born a commoner; that nobility is an accidental quality, while the quality of being a commoner is fundamentally attached to human nature; that nobility, being an acquired title, ought to be personal, and not hereditary, while the quality of being a commoner is both one and the other.

Although nobility is one of the most splendid of distinctions and flatters most the vanity of man, it is nonetheless true that its origin is among the commoners and that it is to the commoners that it owes its creation.

So it is that at the beginning of the French monarchy, dignities and fiefs . . . were revocable; they passed on to the descendants of the possessors only in so far as they inherited their valor and deserved compensation from the state. These rewards of virtue became hereditary only through the weakness of kings and the ambition of subjects who, by the abuse of delegated power, rendered themselves formidable to their masters, and kept what they had usurped.

If everyone agreed that nobility is a virture, how was it possible to decide to make it hereditary and to authorize it as such despite the proof that one sometimes has that nobles are not always the most virtuous of men? If there are a few who follow in the footsteps of their ancestors, there are also some who move away from that virtuous path. If the grandfathers of the latter could come back to life, would they not blush to have produced such fruit, would they not be among the first to cut them off the [family] tree and to kick them into the dirt?

Hereditary nobility having been invented only to perpetuate vanity in families, or better still, only to stimulate the valor of fathers by flattering their vainglory and giving them the hope of seeing perpetuated in their descendants honors acquired through merit, what ought one to think of the laws of certain peoples who never allow one to quit the status to which one is born, however great their acquired merit may be. Are not so injust a set of laws injurious to merit, and visibly harmful to the happiness of society?

It will be objected perhaps that subordination is necessary, that confusion, disorder and contempt would be born of equality, that it was necessary to invent ranks in order to establish good order; that the police of domestic authority gave rise to the idea of a civil police; that the needs of states and of peoples demanded that there be few people to command and many to obey; that if each person did what he wanted to do, such an anarchy [would result as] would be capable of destroying the most populous societies; that although an infinity of hands is necessary in an army, or in public works, a head is, however, needed to direct their operations.

The correctness of these principles will be agreed on without difficulty, but one will always have the right to say that in whatever body merit is found, it alone ought to be honored. It is to ignore the history of mankind and to want to blind oneself to what everyone knows is happening every day to believe that virtue, valor, zeal for country, probity, capacity, talents, experience, scorn of danger, honor in becoming the victim of one's country, the glory of spilling one's blood for her, and, finally, personal merit are always hereditary in families from generation to generation. It is an error of prejudice that men ought to give up. Nobility would not cease to exist if it were not transmissible. The commons would always supply subjects whose transcedent merit would be superior to that of their peers and would bring them special distinctions. It is not persons of merit who are wanting in a state, but places and employments are often wanting to persons of merit.

If there is some difference between the nobility that originated with these great men, which in the course of time has not kept its purity, and commoners enclosed in personal merit, it may, I think, be found only in the fact that the former believes that nothing is capable of measuring up to itself, when ignorance or the misfortune of the ages does not permit it to discover its origin lost in the deepest antiquity; and the latter, ever humble and sheltered from all revolutions, produces titles as incontestable as they are inalterable which, by an unbroken line of ascent, lead back to the first man. The former preciously keeps its charters in its archives, and for a greater security has copies placed in public depositories; the latter, free of all these cares, finds its charters deposited in all families, in all centuries and all ages. The nobility gets no less glory in showing off everywhere its genealogy and in exhibiting the celebrity of its ancestors because it carefully hides their origin; commoners, in whose favor everything speaks, count among their ancestors only manual labor, mediocrity of fortune, probity, simplicity, industry and merit. The noble is born of chance; the commoner is the work of nature. The former is born decorated with honors, without having contributed to them in any way whatsoever, his riches equal his power; the latter carries with him at birth only his disposition to goodness, which he is sometimes happy enough to cultivate, all his work makes him desire only well being, his subordination is reasoned, he conforms in every way to good order, and does not seek to throw off its yoke. The former speaks often of the great deeds of his ancestors, but does not always imitate them; the latter is silent about his forebears' deeds through modesty and, for his own satisfaction or to merit the esteem of others, he seeks opportunities to do new ones. The former shows off his titles, the latter his virtues. The first sometimes sollicits payment for services rendered by their fathers; the second thinks himself too happy when one designs to cast a favorable glance on his own services. To end the comparison, might it not be said, without laying oneself open to the suspicion of being a malevolent critic, that the former is sometimes the last of his line, and the latter the first of his; that one is the shame of his ancestors, the other, the glory of his posterity.

If what we have just noted can happen to the descendants of those famous men who founded their house on the basis of their merit, what ought one to think of the generation of nobles who owe their elevation only to money, which procured for them places of distinction created by the urgent need of the state to provide for its own maintenance? When such a nobility degenerates, can it in good faith be compared to a commons of merit?

THE COMMONS IS THE MOST USEFUL GROUP

The utility of agriculturalists and artisans is too generally recognized for us not to seek to increase their number. Well run nations know their importance more than the others and neglect no means to attract them; they seek to profit from industry and enterprises that are foreign to them; they take from one another in so far as possible, or they benefit from certain circumstances in order to draw to them, both the workers and the new methods in which they excell, because they look upon them as constituting the strength and wealth of their state.

Working people are more useful to a state than those who live in idleness. It is they who carry out all public works and supply personnel for all the arts and crafts. The farmer is the cultivator of his homeland, and the soldier is her defender, and that is why it is impossible to pay too much attention to their maintenance.

In countries where the inhabitants, with the agreement of their sovereign, have a kind of government that suits them, who better than the third estate can know the capacities of a province, determine the quantity of taxes it is in a position to bear, divide them more equitably, see to the construction and maintenance of public roads that are so necessary to the marketing of all sorts of goods; propose to make the rivers easier to cross so as to facilitate greater communications; and last but not least, speak with greater strength for that which is most useful? So it is that this class has the honor of being the first to state its opinion in the meeting of the Estates and of seeing its decisions almost invariably carried out.

The neighboring nation that is so proud of its advantages, so much a rival to our glory, so jealous of its so-called rights and of the chimera of its liberty, what value does she not plate on the commons? And how useful she believes them to be! She does not fear to lose the vain title of her greatness by causing the greatest of her children to learn some mechanical art, either to improve their knowledge or to be able to call on their resources in case some terrible revolution should take place. . . . The House of Commons is always the one whose hidden springs give the greatest movement to affairs of state, whose united deliberations have the greatest weight and best dispose the nation to follow its resolutions.

If experience did not supply us with too many proofs to the contrary, we would not believe that there are nobles who forget their origin to the point of scorning commoners, and of reproaching them their birth. These prideful mortals ought never to erase from their memory that however high or low birth may be, one ought neither to be proud of, nor blush at, it; that condition supposes but does not confer virtues; that, following the example of the Romans, the French ought to base their nobility and their grandeur on love of country and work, and on courage in the face of danger; that, avid for honors, they ought to seek only glory and dispute among themselves only for virtue. They ought to be economical in their household expenditures, loyal to their friends, bold in war, equitable in peace. There is nothing

more out of place than to criticize commoners who distinguish themselves by their worth for the lowliness of their birth.

To how many nobles can commoners say what Marius once said to
the Roman nobility! If you think you have a right to scorn me, do the
same for your ancestors who, like me, owed their nobility to their
virtue. If you envy me the honors with which I have been decorated,
also envy me my probity, my works, the dangers I have faced and
everything that distinguishes me from others. Your pride and your
corruption make you live as if you scorned preferments; your pride
and your ambition make you sollicit them as if they were you due. You
are wrong to claim two things so much the opposite of one another, the
pleasures of laziness and the reward of virtue. Your ancestors left you
everything, with the exception of virtue, because one can neither give
nor receive it. My heroic actions take the place of your honors and
titles. My nobility is not hereditary like yours. I have created it myself
through my labors and the grandeur of my works . . . I know only that
which is useful to the Republic, to defeat its enemies, to defend its
subjects, and to fear nothing but an evil reputation.

16   FROM   *Emmanuel Joseph Sieyès*
                 What Is the Third Estate?

THE THIRD ESTATE IS A COMPLETE NATION

Sieyès first published the pamphlet Qu'est-ce que le tiers état *in January, 1789.*

What does a nation require to survive and prosper? It needs *private*
activities and *public* services.

The private activities can all be comprised within four classes of
persons.

1) Since land and water provide the basic materials for human

SOURCE. Emmanuel Joseph Sieyès, *What Is the Third Estate?*, M. Blondel, trans.
(London: Pall Mall Press Ltd., 1963; New York: Frederick A. Praeger, Inc., 1964),
pp. 53–66, 119–139. Reprinted by permission of the publishers.

needs, the first class, in logical order, includes all the families connected with work on the land.

2) Between the initial sale of goods and the moment when they reach the consumer or user, goods acquire an increased value of a more or less compound nature through the incorporation of varying amounts of labor. In this way human industry manages to improve the gifts of nature and the value of the raw material may be multiplied twice, or ten-fold, or a hundred-fold. Such are the activities of the second class of persons.

3) Between production and consumption, as also between the various stages of production, a variety of intermediary agents intervene, to help producers as well as consumers; these are the dealers and the merchants. Merchants continually compare needs according to place and time and estimate the profits to be obtained from warehousing and transportation; dealers undertake, in the final stage, to deliver the goods on the wholesale and retail markets. Such is the function of the third class of persons.

4) Besides these three classes of useful and industrious citizens who deal with *things* fit to be consumed or used, society also requires a vast number of special activities and of services *directly* useful or pleasant to the *person*. This fourth class embraces all sorts of occupations, from the most distinguished liberal and scientific professions to the lowest of menial tasks.

Such are the activities which support society. But who performs them? The Third Estate.

Public services can also, at present, be divided into four known categories, the army, the law, the Church and the bureaucracy. It needs no detailed analysis to show that the Third Estate everywhere constitutes nineteen-twentieths of them, except that it is loaded with all the really arduous work, all the tasks which the privileged order refuses to perform. Only the well-paid and honorific posts are filled by members of the privileged order. Are we to give them credit for this? We could do so only if the Third Estate was unable or unwilling to fill these posts. We know the answer. Nevertheless, the privileged have dared to preclude the Third Estate. "No matter how useful you are," they said, "no matter how able you are, you can go so far and so further. Honours are not for the like of you." The rare exceptions, noticeable as they are bound to be, are mere mockery, and the sort of language allowed on such occasions is an additional insult.

If this exclusion is a social crime, a veritable act of war against the

Third Estate, can it be said at least to be useful to the common-wealth? Ah! Do we not understand the consequences of monopoly? While discouraging those it excludes, does it not destroy the skill of those it favours? Are we unaware that any work from which free competition is excluded will be performed less well and more expensively?

When any function is made the prerogative of a separate order among the citizens, has nobody remarked how a salary has to be paid not only to the man who actually does the work, but to all those of the same caste who do not, and also to the entire families of both the workers and the non-workers? Has nobody observed that as soon as the government becomes the property of a separate class, it starts to grow out of all proportion and that posts are created not to meet the needs of the governed but of those who govern them? Has nobody noticed that while on the one hand, we basely and I dare say *stupidly* accept this situation of ours, on the other hand, when we read the history of Egypt or stories of travels in India, we describe the same kind of conditions as despicable, monstrous, destructive of all industry, as inimical to social progress, and above all as debasing to the human race in general and intolerable to Europeans in particular . . . ?

It suffices to have made the point that the so-called usefulness of a privileged order to the public service is a fallacy; that, without help from this order, all the arduous tasks in the service are performed by the Third Estate; that without this order the higher posts could be infinitely better filled; that they ought to be the natural prize and reward of recognized ability and service; and that if the privileged have succeeded in usurping all well-paid and honorific posts, this is both a hateful iniquity towards the generality of citizens and an act of treason to the commonwealth.

Who is bold enough to maintain that the Third Estate does not contain within itself everything needful to constitute a complete nation? It is like a strong and robust man with one arm still in chains. If the privileged order were removed, the nation would not be something less but something more. What then is the Third Estate? All; but an "all" that is fettered and oppressed. What would it be without the privileged order? It would be all; but free and flourishing. Nothing will go well without the Third Estate; everything would go considerably better without the two others.

It is not enough to have shown that the privileged, far from being useful to the nation, can only weaken and injure it; we must prove further that the nobility is not part of our society at all: it may be *a burden* for the nation, but it cannot be part of it.

First, it is impossible to find what place to assign to the caste of nobles among all the elements of a nation, I know that there are many people, all too many, who, from infirmity, incapacity, incurable idleness or a collapse of morality, perform no functions at all in society. Exceptions and abuses always exist alongside the rule, and particularly in a large commonwealth. But all will agree that the fewer these abuses, the better organized a state is supposed to be. The most ill-organized state of all would be the one where not just isolated individuals but a complete class of citizens would glory in inactivity amidst the general movement and contrive to consume the best part of the product without having in any way helped to produce it. Such a class, surely, is foreign to the nation because of its *idleness*.

The nobility, however, is also a foreigner in our midst because of its *civil and political* prerogatives.

What is a nation? A body of associates living under *common* laws and represented by the same *legislative assembly,* etc.

Is it not obvious that the nobility possesses privileges and exemptions which it brazenly calls its rights and which stand distinct from the rights of the great body of citizens? Because of these special rights, the nobility does not belong to the common order, nor is it subjected to the common laws. Thus its private rights make it a people apart in the great nation. It is truly *imperium in imperio*.

As for its *political* rights, it also exercises these separately from the nation. It has its own representatives who are charged with no mandate from the People. Its deputies sit separately, and even if they sat in the same chamber as the deputies of ordinary citizens they would still constitute a different and separate representation. They are foreign to the nation first because of their origin, since they do not owe their powers to the People; and secondly because of their aim, since this consists in defending, not the general interest, but the private one.

The Third Estate then contains everything that pertains to the nation while nobody outside the Third Estate can be considered as part of the nation. What is the Third Estate? *Everything*.

WHAT HAS THE THIRD ESTATE BEEN UNTIL NOW? NOTHING

We shall examine neither the condition of servitude in which the People has suffered for so long, nor that of constraint and humiliation in which it is still confined. Its status has changed in private law. It must change still further: the nation as a whole cannot be free, nor can any of its separate orders, unless the Third Estate is free. Freedom does not derive from privileges. It derives from the rights of citizens—and these rights belong to all.

If the aristocrats try to repress the People at the expense of that very freedom of which they prove themselves unworthy, the Third Estate will dare challenge their right. If they reply, "by the right of conquest," one must concede that this is to go back rather far. Yet the Third Estate need not fear examining the past. It will betake itself to the year preceding the "conquest"; and as it is nowadays too strong to be conquered it will certainly resist effectively. Why should it not repatriate to the Franconian forests all the families who wildly claim to descend from the race of the conquerors and to inherit their *rights of conquest*?

If it were purged in this way, I think the nation might well recover from the thought that thenceforward it would be reduced to the descendants of mere Gauls and Romans. When our poor fellow-citizens insist on distinguishing between one lineage and another, could nobody reveal to them that it is at least as good to be descended from the Gauls and the Romans as from the Sicambrians, Welches and other savages from the woods and swamps of ancient Germany? "True enough," some will say; "but conquest has upset all relationships and hereditary nobility now descends through the line of the conquerors." Well, then; we shall have to arrange for it to descend through the other line! The Third Estate will become noble again by becoming a conqueror in its own turn.

But, if we accept that all races are mixed; if the blood of the Franks (none the better for being pure) now mingles with the blood of the Gauls; if the fathers of the Third Estate are the fathers of the whole nation; can we not hope that one day will see the end of this long parricide which one class is proud to commit day after day against all the others? Why should not reason and justice, eventually grown as powerful as vanity, press so hard upon the privileged order that, moved by a new, truer and more social interest, it requests its own *regeneration* within the order of the Third Estate?[1]

---

[1] In the First Edition this paragraph ran thus: "If we see in the privileged order, which is the constant enemy of the Third Estate, that which is alone in fact observable there, viz. the children of this same Third Estate, how are we to describe the parricidal audacity with which the privileged hate, despise and oppress their brothers?"

Let us pursue our theme. By Third Estate is meant all the citizens who belong to the common order. Anybody who holds a legal privilege of any kind deserts the common order, stands as an exception to the common laws and, consequently, does not belong to the Third Estate. As we have already said, a nation is made one by virtue of common laws and common representation. It is indisputably only too true that in France a man who is protected only by the common laws is a nobody; whoever is totally unprivileged must submit to every form of contempt, insult and humiliation. To avoid being completely crushed, what must the unlucky non-priviliged person do? He has to attach himself by all kinds of contemptible actions to some magnate; he prostitutes his principles and human dignity for the possibility of claiming, in his need, the protection of a *somebody*.

But we are less concerned in this book with the civil rights of the Third Estate than with its relationship to the constitution. Let us see what part it plays in the States-General.

Who have been its so-called "Representatives"? Men who have been raised to the nobility or have received temporary privileges. These bogus deputies have not even been always freely elected by the People. In the States-General sometimes, and in the Provincial Estates almost always, the representation of the People is considered as inherent in the holder of certain offices.

The old aristocracy detests new nobles; it allows nobles to sit as such only when they can prove, as the phrase goes, "four generations and a hundred years." Thus it relegates the other nobles to the order of the Third Estate to which, obviously, they no longer belong.

In law, however, all nobles are equal—those whose nobility dates from yesterday just as much as those who succeed for better or for worse in hiding their origins or their usurpation. In law all have the same privileges. Only *opinion* distinguishes between them. But if the Third Estate must endure a prejudice sanctioned by law, there is no reason why it should submit to a prejudice contrary to law.

Let them create as many noblemen as they like; it still remains certain that the moment any citizen is granted privileges against the common laws, he no longer forms part of the common order. His new interest is contrary to the general interest; he becomes incompetent to vote in the name of the People.

According to the same undeniable principle, those who merely hold temporary privileges must also be debarred from representing the Third Estate. Their interest, too, is in greater or lesser part opposed to the common interest; and although opinion assigns them to the Third

Estate and the law does not mention them, the nature of things, stronger than both opinion and the law, sets them irresistibly apart from the common order.

It is objected that to remove from the Third Estate not only those with hereditary privileges, but even those with mere temporary ones, is to try, from sheer wantonness, to weaken that order by depriving it of its more enlightened, courageous and esteemed members.

The last thing I want to do is to diminish the strength or dignity of the Third Estate, since, in my mind, it is completely coincident with my idea of a nation. But can we, whatever our motives, arrange for truth to cease to be truth? If an army has the misfortune to be deserted by its best soldiers, are these the troops it entrusts with the defence of its camp? One cannot say it too often: any privilege runs contrary to common laws; hence, all those who enjoy privileges, without exception, constitute a separate class opposed to the Third Estate. At the same time, I must point out that this should not alarm the friends of the People. On the contrary, it takes us back to the higher national interest by showing the urgent necessity for immediately suppressing all temporary privileges which split the Third Estate and may seem to oblige it to put its destiny in its enemies' hands. Besides, this remark must not be separated from the ensuing one: the abolition of privileges within the Third Estate does not mean the loss of immunities which some of its members enjoy. Such immunities are nothing but common rights and it was totally unjust to deprive the main part of the People of them. Thus, I am not calling for the loss of a right but for its restitution, and should it be objected that the universalization of certain privileges—e.g. not balloting for militia service—would make it impossible to satisfy various public needs, my answer is that any public need is the responsibility of everybody and not of a separate class of citizens, and that one must be as ill-acquainted with reasoning as with fairness if one cannot think of a more national means of constituting and maintaining whatever kind of army one wants to have.

Consequently, either because they were never elected at all; or because they were not elected by the full membership of the Third Estate of towns and rural areas who were entitled to representation; or because, owing to their privileges, they were not even eligible; the so-called deputies of the Third Estate who have sat until now in the States-General never had a real mandate from the People.[2]

[2]This paragraph did not appear in the First Edition.

Some occasionally express surprise at hearing complaints about a three-fold "astocracy composed of the army, the Church and the law." They insist that this is only a figure of speech; yet the phrase must be understood strictly. If the States-General is the interpreter of the general will, and correspondingly has the right to make laws, it is this capacity, without doubt, that makes it a true aristocracy: whereas the States-General as we know it at present is simply a *clerico-nobili-judicial* assembly.

Add to this appalling truth the fact that, in one way or another, all departments of the executive have also fallen into the hands of the caste that provides the Church, the law and the army. As a result of a spirit of brotherhood or *comradeship*, nobles always prefer each other to the rest of the nation. The usurpation is total; in every sense of the word, they reign.

If you consult history in order to verify whether the facts agree or disagree with my description, you will discover, as I did, that it is a great mistake to believe that France is a monarchy. With the exception of a few years under Louis XI and under Richelieu and a few moments under Louis XIV when it was plain despotism, you will believe you are reading the history of a *Palace* aristocracy. It is not the King who reigns; it is the Court. The Court has made and the Court has unmade; the Court has appointed ministers and the Court has dismissed them; the Court has created posts and the Court has filled them. . . . And what is the Court but the head of this vast aristocracy which overruns every part of France, which seizes on everything through its members, which exercises everywhere every essential function in the whole administration? So that in its complaints the People has grown used to distinguishing between the monarch and those who exercise power. It has always considered the King as so certainly misled and so defenceless in the midst of the active and all-powerful Court, that it has never thought of blaming him for all the wrongs done in his name.

Finally, is it not enough simply to open our eyes to what is occurring around us at this very moment? What do we see? The aristocracy on its own, fighting simultaneously against reason, justice, the People, the minister and the King. The end of this terrible battle is still undecided. Can it still be said that the aristocracy is only a chimera!

Let us sum up: to this very day, the Third Estate has never had genuine representatives in the States-General. Thus its political rights are null.

WHAT OUGHT TO HAVE BEEN DONE? BASIC PRINCIPLES

In every free nation, and every nation ought to be free, there is only one way of settling disputes about the constitution. One must not call upon Notables, but upon the nation itself. If we have no constitution, it must be made, and only the nation has the right to make it. If we do have a constitution, as some people obstinately maintain, and if, as they allege, it divides the National Assembly into three deputations of three orders of citizens, nobody can fail to notice, at all events, that one of these orders is protesting so vigorously that nothing can be done until its claim is decided. Now, who has the right to judge in such a matter?

A question of this nature could only seem unimportant to those who disparage just and natural methods of handling social affairs and put their trust in the factitious qualities, usually rather undesirable and devious, on which the reputations of so-called statesmen, the alleged "leading politicians," are based. As for us, we shall not deviate from the moral rule; morality must determine all the relationships which bind men to each other, both in their private interests and in their common or social interest. Morality must point out the way for us; and, after all, only morality can do so. We must always go back to basic principles for they are more cogent than all the achievements of genius.

We shall never understand social machinery unless we examine a society as though it were an ordinary machine. It is necessary to consider each part of it separately, and then link them all together in the mind in due order, to see how they fit together and hear the general harmony that necessarily follows. . . . We shall at least ask the reader to distinguish three periods in the making of a political society, and these distinctions will pave the way for such explanation as is necessary.

In the first period, we assume a fairly considerable number of isolated individuals who wish to unite; by this fact alone, they already constitute a nation: they enjoy all the rights of a nation and it only remains for them to exercise them. This first period is characterized by the activity of the *individual* wills. The association is their work; they are the origin of all power.

The second period is characterized by the action of the *common* will. The associates want to give consistency to their union; they want to fulfil its aim. They therefore discuss and agree amongst themselves on public needs and on ways of satisfying them. We see that power, then,

belongs to the community. Individual wills still constitute its origin
and form its essential components; but, taken separately, they would
be powerless. Power exists only in the aggregate. The community
needs a common will; without *singleness* of will it could not succeed in
being a willing and acting body. It is certain, also, that this body has
no rights other than such as derive from the common will.

But let us leap the lapse of time. The associates are now too
numerous and occupy too large an area to exercise their commom
will easily by themselves. What do they do? They separate out whatever is necessary to attend to and satisfy public requirements; and they
put a few of their number in charge of exercising this portion of the
national will, that is to say this portion of power. We have now
reached the third period, the period of *government by proxy*. Let us
point out a few facts: 1) The community does not cast aside its right
to will: this is inalienable; it can only delegate the exercise of that
right. This principle is elaborated elsewhere. 2) Nor can it delegate the
full exercise of it. It delegates only that portion of its total power
which is needed to maintain order. In this matter, no more is sur-
rendered than necessary. 3) Therefore, it does not rest with the body
of delegates to alter the limits of the power that has been entrusted to
them. Obviously such a competence would be self-contradictory.

I distinguish the third period from the second in that it is no longer
the *real* common will which is in operation, but a *representative* common will. It has two ineffiaceable characteristics which we must repeat.
1) This will which resides in the body of representatives is neither
complete nor unlimited; it is a mere portion of the grand, common,
national will. 2) The delegates do not exercise it as a right inherent
in themselves, but as a right pertaining to other people; the common
will is confided to them in trust.

For the moment I put aside a mass of problems which this discussion naturally gives rise to, and go straight on. What is meant by the
political constitution of a society? And what is its exact relationship
to the nation itself?

It is impossible to create a body for any purpose without giving
it the organization, procedures and laws appropriate for it to fulfil
its intended functions. This is called the *constitution* of this body.
Obviously, the body cannot exist without it. Therefore, it is equally
obvious that every government must have its constitution; and what
is true for the government in general is true for each of its components.
Thus the Assembly of Representatives which is entrusted with the
legislative power, i.e. the exercise of the common will, exists only in

the form which the nation has chosen to give it. It is nothing outside the articles of its constitution; only through its constitution can it act, conduct its proceedings and govern. . . .

. . . *What ought to have been done* amidst all the difficulties and disputes about the coming States-General? Should we have convened No-tables? No. Should we have let the nation and its interests languish? No. Should we have exercised diplomacy upon the interested parties to persuade them all to compromise? No. We should have resorted to the extreme measure of calling an extraordinary representative body. It is the nation that ought to have been consulted.

Let us answer two questions which still remain. Where is the nation to be found? Whose function is it to consult the nation?

1) Where is the nation to be found? Where it is; in the 40,000 parishes which embrace the whole territory, all its inhabitants and every element of the commonwealth; indisputably, the nation lies there. A geographical division would have been chosen so that "*arrondissements*" of 20 to 30 parishes could easily form and elect first deputies. Along similar lines, "*arrondissements*" would have formed provinces; and the provinces would have sent to the capital authentic extraordinary representatives with special powers to decide upon the constitution of the States-General.

You object that this procedure would have entailed too much delay? Surely no more than the succession of expedients which have simply led to further confusion. Besides, it was not a question of saving time, but of adopting workable measures to achieve the aim. Had people been willing and able to stick to true principles, more could have been done for the nation in four months than the progress of enlightenment and public opinion, powerful none the less as I believe it to be, could do in half a century.

But, if the *majority* of the citizens had nominated extraordinary representatives, what would have happened, you may ask, to the distinction between the three orders? What would have become of privileges? They would have become what they deserve to be. The principles which I have just recited are certainties. Abandon the hope of having social order, or else accept these principles. The nation is always free to amend its constitution. Above all, it cannot absolve itself from the responsibility of giving certainty to a disputed con-stitution. Everybody agrees on that to-day; cannot you see, then, that the nation could not interfere if it were itself merely a participant in the dispute? A body subjected to constitutional forms cannot take any decision outside the scope of its constitution. It cannot give itself another one. It becomes null and void from the moment when it moves, speaks or acts in any other than the prescribed forms. Even if the States-General were already in session, it would therefore be incompetent to decide upon the constitution. Such a right belongs only to the nation which, we continue to reiterate, is independent of any procedure and any qualifications.

As is obvious, the privileged classes have good reasons for befogging the concepts and principles which relate to this matter. They are boldly prepared to-day to uphold the opposite of the views they were advocating six months ago. At that time there was a single outcry in France: we had no constitution and we asked for one to be made. To-day, we not only have a constitution but, if we are to believe the privileged classes, one which contains two excellent and unchallengeable provisions. The first is the *division* of the citizens *into orders*; the second is the *equality of influence* of each order in the formation of the national will. We have already sufficiently proved that even if both these elements were indeed comprised in our constitution, the nation would always be free to change them. It remains to examine more particularly the nature of this *equality* of influence that they seek to attribute to each order in the formation of the national will. We shall see that such an idea is impossibly absurd and that no nation could possibly include anything of the kind in its constitution.

A political society cannot be anything but the whole body of the associates. A nation cannot decide not to be the nation, or to be so only in a certain fashion: for that would be saying that it is not the nation in any other fashion. Similarly, a nation cannot decree that its common will shall cease to be its common will. It is sad to have to state facts which may appear so simple as to be silly, until one thinks of the conclusions they entail. It follows that no nation has ever been able to decree that the rights inherent in the common will, i.e. in the majority, should pass into the hands of the minority. The common will cannot destroy itself. It cannot change the nature of things, nor arrange that the opinion of the minority shall be the opinion of the majority. Clearly such a regulation would not be a legal or a moral act: it would be lunacy.

Consequently if it be claimed that under the French constitution two hundred thousand individuals out of twenty-six million citizens constitute two-thirds of the common will, only one comment is possible: it is a claim that two and two make five.

The sole elements of the common will are individual wills. One can neither deny the greatest number the right to play their part, nor decide that these ten wills are equivalent to only one while another ten wills amount to thirty. These are contradictions in terms, pure absurdities.

If for the slightest moment one loses sight of this self-evident principle that the common will is the opinion of the majority and not of the minority, there is no point in carrying on the discussion. One might just as well decide that the will of a single man is to be called majority and that we no longer need States-General or national will at all. For, if the will of a nobleman can be worth as much as ten wills, why should not the will of a minister be worth as much as a hundred? a million? twenty-six million? On the basis of this reasoning, all the national deputies may as well be sent home and every demand of the People suppressed.

Is it necessary to insist further on the logical deduction from these principles? It is a certainty that among the national representatives, whether ordinary or extraordinary, influence must be proportionate to the number of citizens who have the *right* to be represented. If it is to accomplish its task, the representative body must always be the substitute for the nation itself. It must partake of the same *nature*, the same *proportions* and the same *rules*.

To conclude: these principles are all self-consistent and prove: a) only an extraordinary representative body can establish or amend the constitution; b) this constituent representative body must be set up without regard to the distinction between orders.

2) Whose function is it to consult the nation? If the constitution provides for a legislature, each of its component parts would have the right to consult the nation, just as litigants are always allowed to appeal to the courts; or, rather, because the interpreters of a will are obliged to consult with those who appointed them to seek explanations about their mandate or to give notice of circumstances requiring new powers. But for almost two centuries we have been without representatives—even assuming that we had them at that time. Since we have none, who is going to take their place vis-à-vis the nation? Who is going to inform the People of the need for extraordinary representatives? This question will embarrass only those who attach to the word "convening" the hotchpotch of English ideas. We are not talking here of the royal *prerogative*, but of the simple and natural meaning of "convening." This word embraces: *notice* as to the national necessity and *designation* of a common meeting place. Well then, when the preservation of the motherland harries every citizen, is time to be

wasted inquiring who has the *right* to convene the assembly? Ask, rather: who has not such a right? It is the sacred *duty* of all those who can do something about it. *A fortiori*, the executive is qualified to do it; for it is in a better position than private individuals to give notice to the whole nation, to designate the place of the assembly and to sweep aside all the obstructions of corporate interests. The Prince indubitably, in so far as he is the first citizen, has a greater interest than anyone else in convoking the People. He may not be competent to decide on the constitution, but it is impossible to say that he is incompetent to bring such a decision about.

So it is not difficult to answer the question, "what ought to have been done?" The nation ought to have been convened, so as to send to the capital extraordinary representatives with a special mandate to frame the constitution for the ordinary National Assembly. I would have objected to such representatives having the power to sit in the ordinary assembly as well. This ordinary assembly would be operating under the constitution which they had themselves drawn up in their previous capacity; hence my fear lest, instead of confining themselves to the national interest alone, they might pay too much attention to the body of which they were about to become members. In politics, it is the mingling and confusion of powers that constantly make it impossible to establish social order anywhere in the world; by the same token, the moment it is decided to separate what ought to be distinct, the great problem of organizing a human society for the general welfare of its members will be successfully solved.

17 FROM *F. Y. Besnard*
Souvenirs d'un Nonagénaire

Our ancestors of both sexes called *Demoiselle* only the wives of the highest placed men in society; and the name of *Monsieur* applied only only to those men whose fortune or profession easily set them apart from the rest of the population.

All others were known as master or mistress. Members of the

SOURCE. F. Y. Besnard, *Souvenirs d'un Nonagénaire* (Paris: Librairie H. Champion, 1880), I, pp. 48–50, 126–130, 135–137, 142–144, 200–201. Translated for this volume by Susan Kaplow.

working class simply went by their family or first names. They considered themselves offended or derided if anyone addressed them by them otherwise than by their names alone.

The heads of household, especially in the bourgeoisie, rarely failed to appear at the high mass of the parish accompanied by their children. Each one of them had his private pew and only turned out very carefully dressed.

It was not exactly the same as regards Vespers, although some took it as their duty or their custom to attend this service. It was really the turn of the female servants, who for the most part had only been able to hear a low mass.

On Sunday and holidays, the shops were closed, all menial labor was generally suspended, and everyone stayed home in a state of perfect repose.

Days of abstinence and of fasting were scrupulously observed. During Lent, meat could be sold by no butchers except those who, in order to obtain permission to do so, had contracted at the time of bidding to give the highest amount to the hospitals.

Social gatherings were few and rare. Only two or three houses in the town of Doué had any: Those of the Delavau and of the Bineau. They were held almost always on Sunday, following Vespers. After very light refreshments, they would play at darts or at [card games]. At eight o'clock in the evening everyone returned home. This was also more or less the case in the larger cities.

At that time, only eight or ten families in the entire city [of Angers] had vehicles, that is to say carriages, and one rarely saw them moving about. They were only light basket affairs, like those which Parisian carriage drivers had until the beginning of the nineteenth century.

The horses which were harnessed to them were very little like those of today's post masters and rarely were worth more than 500 to 600 francs each. They were primarily used to transport their masters from town to country and, in the country, to their different acquaintances in the area.

The cabriolets were ordinarily just simple buggies to which were harnessed horses worth 200 or 300 francs each. The number of these was proportionally as limited as that of the carriages. Thus families which owned them rarely used them either for visiting, or for going to church or promenades.

But when they went to these places, they had themselves attended by a servant in livery called a footman. There were very few of these footmen. I saw as many as three or four only with Monseigneur the

Bishop and with the Marquis de la Loire, the only ones who also ventured to have valets.

Not only nobles and high magistrates, but also many bourgeois families, had chateaux and country houses at more or less great distances from the city. Except for those impeded by their business or the duties of their professions, all these owners hurried to their properties as soon after the end of the Fair of the Consecration—Corpus Christi—as possible. This fair attracted to the city and retained there crowds of strangers.

The others left one after the other, so that at the beginning of the vacation period the city seemed to be no more than a desert compared to its animated state a short time before. At this time, every day saw some of these families pass by in traveling clothes, ambling along on horses led by their farmers or sharecroppers. Accustomed to wearing pack-saddles, they were only able to walk slowly.

Sometimes the husbands and the male children old enough to bear the fatigue accompanied the ladies and the cook on foot, along with the farmers. The youngest of both sexes mounted double behind the riders.

The lack of major roads, the poor condition of the thoroughfares, scarcely allowed of any other means of leaving the town. Thus even the wealthiest persons kept saddle-horses in it but rarely.

The wages of trained cooks, like those of male domestics, were modest. It was, at least, unusual for them to rise above 100 francs [per year], and only a few had a salary which reached this figure.

In the lower classes of society, marriages did not usually take place until age thirty or even later. This was especially true of domestics in the towns and in the countryside. Conversely, they commonly occurred among the wealthy at age 20 or 25. A son was considered a confirmed bachelor at age 26 or 27. I well remember that the one thing people criticized in the marriages of my sister and of my cousin Vallée was that the intended of the former was 26 while she was but 21, and the intended of the latter was 27 while she was but 20.

Although domestic servants of both sexes were few in number in each house, far from being overburdened with work, they seemed to lack any for a large part of the day. The reason for this was, that in the absence of sumptuous furnishings, they did not have to bother with polishing the floor, or with cleaning and sweeping all the things which today adorn the different rooms of an apartment.

At this time, Angers had only one banker. There was not a single millionaire among the merchants nor even among the nobles, excepting the Marquis de la Loire and Monsieur de Giseux, whose only daughter was married to the Duc de Brancas. The largest dowries, with extremely few exceptions and only in the most important noble families, did not rise above 20,000 francs. Those of 10,000 francs caused a stir in the town.

People willingly retired from business when they acquired an income of 3,000 or 4,000 livres; this was considered by the entire third estate to be a very respectable fortune. It was then a commonly held opinion that anyone who could not live on 3,000 livres could not live on 100,000.

Men and women of the upper and middle classes scarcely ever left their houses without having had their hair and wigs curled and powdered white. Monks and members of the lower classes did not allow themselves this type of luxury except (and this applies only to the latter) in very extraordinary circumstances. These individuals dressed in manner which clearly differentiated them from persons of higher social position.

At this time, clothes passed from father to child and from older to younger brother, after having been pulled apart and cut down to smaller size. For this type of work, and almost always for the making new garments as well, tailors were employed by the day.

The best bourgeois, lawyers, doctors, notaries, etc., ordinarily ate in their kitchens at this time. When they had guests, the meal was generally served in the "company" parlor, as dining rooms were found only in a very small number of houses.

Beds were placed in almost all the rooms of a dwelling and were 4 feet wide and sometimes more. Four columns held up the frame and rods designed to support full curtains, which were usually made of green or yellow material. But the columns gradually disappeared from bourgeois houses. Then, the frame and the curtains were hung from the ceiling by means of a rope and a hook; thus the beds came to be called angel beds. Their width allowed two or three persons to sleep together and we know that husbands and wives used to share the same bed, as did two or three children of the same age.

Fashions did change at times, but only after a period of four, five, six years, or even longer.

Custom had set the dress and appearance of individuals to such an extent that members of the upper and lower classes of the population were easily distinguishable one from another. And within the lower classes, certain nuances were so pronounced that at first sight one could tell the condition or the profession of any person.

Thus the dress of a female servant or cook was not the same as that of a chambermaid nor, with all the more reason, the same as that of her mistress. Nor was the journeyman's the same as the master's, the small shopkeeper's the same as the cloth merchant's, or as the goldsmith's or the jeweler's.

And even less so, were these the same as the dress of the bourgeois, that is of the man who had no profession and lived on the product of his investments. Only people of this latter type were considered bourgeois, just as nobles who engaged in certain occupations or in any branch of commerce were thought to have derogated from their class.

Nobles and other privileged persons who had the right to do so almost never appeared in the street without their swords at their sides, hanging horizontally from their belts. Their hats were trimmed with gold braid and often adorned with plumes.

Workers employed as journeymen by masters such as cobblers, tailors, carpenters, smiths, bakers, etc., generally receive a monthly wage of 6 or sometimes 8 francs. But they were lodged and fed. At this time, one rarely saw them at cabarets, where, on the other hand, their masters often could be found.

In those days, the highest magistrates and the most distinguished lawyers of the city went about with their caps on their heads, decked out in great wigs in the style of Louis XV or with their hair well powdered. Both came down to the middle of their backs and ended in two or three spirals of curls.

One could see these men return solemnly from the law court and, nearing their homes, search in the folds of their ample robes for the keys with which to open their doors. These doors were rarely carriage-entrances. . . . They had a smaller door within one of their leaves or to the side.

These different types of doors . . . sometimes opened onto a small courtyard. More frequently, they led into a vestibule where the doors to the ground-floor rooms were to be found. There also was the spiral staircase, made of wooden planks or of slate, and leading to the upper floors; and the staircase which led to the basement.

In those days, most artisans lived in cramped quarters. Outside of their shops or workrooms, they often lived in one large room, which was at once kitchen, dining room, and family bedroom. There was also another room for the journeymen whom they lodged and fed.

The salary of these journeymen was quite low; it rarely exceeded 6 francs a month in most trades. Indeed for wigmakers' assistants, it was limited to whatever small change they received from the customers they were charged with serving.

With very few exceptions, dressmakers and seamstresses did very little of their work at home. Usually they worked in the homes of private parties who hired them by the day for six sous. From this came the practice of referring to them in way of a jest by the nickname of *six sous*.

IV THE URBAN WORKERS
AND THE POOR

Industrial capitalism was practically unknown in eighteenth century France. There was, therefore, no proletariat in the modern sense of the term. Instead, there were artisans of all sorts, both independent and dependant, in and outside the guilds. Those in the guilds were normally the most skilled and enjoyed the best standard of living, although this varied from guild to guild and city to city. The others—street merchants, unskilled day laborers, domestic servants—lived, in the main, in a kind of perpetual poverty, which the economic crisis on the eve of the Revolution made intolerable.

The guild was not really the forerunner of the modern trade union, although there are superficial resemblances between the two, specifically since both are organizations of producers whose purpose it is to defend their corporate interests. The guilds were run by and for the masters, who attained that status only after serving terms as apprentices and journeymen. Theoretically, all artisans could some day expect to become masters, but in practice they often spent their lives as journeymen, the more so as one approaches the end of the old regime. This was because the masters, increasingly subject to the control of merchant capitalists, contrived to protect themselves by limiting the grant of mastership to their own sons and relations. Although masters and journeymen often acted in concert against outsiders, there were more and more frequent disputes between the two groups as the old regime drew to a close.

The apprentice was expected to give loyal service to his master for a period of years, usually three to seven. In return, he was instructed in the skills of the trade. Sometimes the contract called for the payment of a fee to the master. The apprentice normally lived in the master's house, and the master stood *in loco parentis* to him. The relationship between the master, on the one hand, and apprentices and journeymen, on the other, was not restricted to the payment of money in return for labor, as in modern industrial capitalism. The pattern was, rather, one of hierarchical subordination after the model of the patriarchal family sanctioned by Catholic practice. The duties of an apprentice are here outlined by Jacques Savary (1622–1690), who was a mercer of noble origin and whose family had been in trade since the sixteenth century. He was often called on by the government of Louis XIV to give advice on commercial matters, so much so that he gave his name to the mercantile code embodied in the law of 1673. Although written in 1675, this conception of the apprentice's duty was valid throughout the eighteenth century. The same is true of the statutes of the locksmiths' guild of Paris, drafted in 1650.

In response to the attempts by masters to control closely all aspects of work and production, the journeymen (*compagnons*) organized themselves separately to protect their interests. The origin of these *compagnonnages* is difficult, if not impossible, to ascertain, shrouded as they are in a variety of legends. We do know that twenty-seven trades were organized in three rival groups at the Revolution. They were the *Enfants du Père Soubise*, the *Enfants du Maître Jacques* and the *Enfants du Salomon*. Their rivalry was intense and sometimes led to bloodshed. Each exercised close discipline over its members as they wandered from city to city on the *Tour de France* with the aim of improving their skills. Employment and wages were subject to regulation by the compagnonnages, and they were known to call strikes and to blacklist both employers and workers who did not do as they wished. Ritual initiation was a common practice, the intent being to protect the members of these illegal associations by threatening them with vengeance and retribution should they fail to do their duty or should they betray the secrets of the fellowship. The ritual also served as a powerful force to bind men together by conferring a quasisacred character on their activities, and it is eloquent testimony to their profound, if syncretic Christianity. The authorities were much concerned with their ritual and activities, not only because of the blasphemy that was involved in the former, but because they considered any organization of workingmen to be dangerous to the peace and tranquility of society. The condemnation of their practices by the

Faculty of Theology of the Sorbonne spells out their fears in so many words, as does the police ordinance issued in Nantes more than one hundred years later.

The next selections describe the living conditions of that great mass of the urban population that made its living outside the guilds. As previously stated, they were often much worse off than the skilled artisans. With the possible exception of the Île de la Cité, the Faubourg Saint Marcel was the area of most dire poverty in Paris, much more so than the artisanal center of the Faubourg Saint Antoine. The inhabitants were ever at the mercy of a sudden rise in bread prices, underemployment, or the loss of a job. Drunkenness and religious fervor, both of which serve to make one forget the misery of reality, were the order of the day. Unable to strike out at the real causes of evil conditions, the men and women of this district turned on one another with insults, threats, and assaults. Private life became public, and all were called to bear witness against the transgressor, who might be anyone but the constituted authorities. The description of the quarter here translated is by Louis Sebastien Mercier (1740–1814), a minor philosophe, playwright, and republican politician who ended his life as a member of the newly created Institut de France. His remarks are seconded by the account of Friedrich Schulz, a German traveller who visited Paris in 1789.

Schulz may very well have been correct in asserting that but for the shortage of bread, the *menu peuple* would have shown little interest in revolution. But the lack of food does not sufficiently explain why a series of bread riots came to have such great revolutionary potential. In order to find an adequate explanation, the mental sets of the laboring poor must be taken into account. What they believed and how their beliefs affected their behavior is of the utmost importance. This is largely unexplored territory. Barbier and Mercier describe their superstition and dependance on at least the outward manifestations of religion. Their reports make an excellent starting point for our own speculations and, hopefully, research.

18 FROM *Jacques Savary*
Le Parfait Negociant

OF THE WAY IN WHICH APPRENTICES IN THE RETAIL TRADES SHOULD CONDUCT THEMSELVES IN THEIR MASTERS' HOUSES, AND WHAT THEY SHOULD LEARN DURING THEIR APPRENTICESHIP

The first thing that an apprentice should have in view is love and fear of God, without which God will not bless his work, and he will never succeed in his undertakings. One must love Him and serve Him, and to do so, the apprentice should go to mass daily if he can. He finds ample facility and opportunity to do so in his comings and goings around town; and those who are obliged to spend great lengths of time in their stores and shops can get up a half-hour earlier in the morning.

Far from condemning this practice, masters will approve of it, because it guarantees them good conduct. Indeed, there are some merchants, men of piety, who send their servants—both those in the shop and the domestics—everyday to hear mass. Anyone failing to do this would be chased from the house.

The apprentice should also follow the good and ancient custom of going to the parish mass on Sundays with his masters. Less than thirty years ago, all merchants still followed this practice. But today, masters have become lax because most of them are as dissolute as their apprentices, and so the disturbances that trouble us daily should not surprise us.

The second thing that an apprentice must have is loyalty to his masters. To this he is bound by his contract of apprenticeship, which usually states that he will work to the advantage of his masters and avoid harming him.

Not only does this mean that he will serve faithfully, but also that he will stop friends, servants, domestics, or anyone else from injuring his master. His conscience as well as his contract obliges him to do so.

SOURCE. Jacques Savary, *Le Parfait Négociant* (Paris: new enlarged edition by Philémont-Louis Savary, 1757, originally published 1675), I, Book I, pp. 41–46. Translated for this volume by Susan Kaplow.

The third thing is blind obedience to his master, provided that what he is ordered to do offends neither God nor his conscience. In such a case, he ought not to obey.

An apprentice should not look for the motives behind his master's commands. However, something clearly unreasonable may occasionally be demanded of him. For example, a master in his anger might tell him to deliver a nasty message to someone, or to do something similar. If he thinks that his master, once calmed, might be damaged by the consequences, the apprentice should not obey promptly but should wait for the order to be repeated. In this case, it is rendering a good service not to obey orders, and the disobedience is advantageous.

It may also happen that a master, saying one thing for another, commands something which is contrary to the welfare of his business. When this happens, the apprentice should pretend to have heard incorrectly and ask the master if he did not mean such and such thing.

If he repeats the same order, the apprentice may, with due respect, point out to him what damage to his business may result. Then, if the master still desires his original command to be executed, he must obey without rejoinder or murmur.

The fourth thing which an apprentice must have is a great respect for his master, speaking to him only with hat in hand, as if he were his father; since he cares for his up-bringing like a father while the apprentice is under his supervision. In the apprenticeship contract it says that they should act as befits good fathers.

It is not a shameful lowering of oneself to speak to the master hat in hand, but a seemly duty becoming well-breed persons. In England, apprentices are still more humble than in France. For, though gentlemen and sometimes brothers of lords, they are always bareheaded in the store or shop, and eat standing up at their masters' tables. In many cities of the realm, such as Toulouse and Bordeaux, the apprentices follow these English customs. It is certain that the more humble and respectful they are toward their masters, the more they will be considered upright individuals.

The fifth thing is to keep the master's affairs secret, and never divulge them to anyone. This is very important for the maintenance of his business, either in buying or selling; there might even be something which would ruin him if let out.

The sixth thing is to live on good terms with comrades, and other servants of the house. There should be no quarreling or fighting— these being the actions of lowlifes and not of children of the same family. Particularly, there should be no tale-telling to the master, unless about something concerning his interests.

The apprentice should live with modesty, avoid drunkenness and the company of those given to loose-living and debauchery. Not to do so would wipe out his good reputation and might involve him in evil dealings which would cause his utter ruin.

The seventh and last thing is to dress modestly but cleanly. It is a strange and shameful thing today to see apprentices and salesman dressed like lords: one could often mistake them for the masters of the house, and the masters for the factors. That the masters permit this is surprising and thus one cannot pity them when the factors rob them in order to maintain their luxurious and superfluous style of dressing.

Having spoken of the way of life of the apprentice in his master's house, we must discuss what he will have to do during the period of his apprenticeship to prepare himself for retail commerce.[1]

The first thing which the apprentice has to know is the mark or figure which the master uses to indicate the price of the merchandise in the store or shop. Without this, he would be unable to sell it.

Second, are the weights and measures, to measure out . . . and weigh the merchandise. Without knowing these perfectly, even to the smallest of them, he cannot sell and debit; he will not become a master in the guild and in the community until he has been questioned on these matters.

The third task to which the apprentice must apply himself is to learning where the goods are stored, to be able to find them in their exact location, when the master asks for them. This is necessary so as not to make merchants lose patience or to force them to go elsewhere because they are not promptly served.

He should remember how to handle and fold the merchandise properly to avoid damaging or spoiling it. This is what we mean by sparing the master harm, which is an obligation set down in the apprenticeship contract.

The fourth thing the apprentice must do is to acquire a knowledge of the different sorts of merchandise. He should not be ashamed to ask his master or his comrades about the quality or defectiveness of the goods, about the origins of any flaws which buyers may have re-marked in them and which kept them from being sold.

[1] It goes without saying that these recommendations were meant to apply, *mutatis mutandis*, to apprentice artisans as well as apprentice traders.

He will also find out from which countries the merchandise comes, whether from within the realm or from foreign lands. He should ask whether the master buys it first hand in the workshop where it is made or manufactured; whether he buys it for cash or on credit; how much more it costs on credit.

In addition, the apprentice must also acquaint himself with the width and length of the goods and with the differing qualities thereof.

The fifth thing is to learn to make packages and bundles well so that the wares are preserved and not spoiled when they arrive in the provinces or foreign countries to which they are sent.

The sixth thing is to acquire perfection in the selling of merchandise. It is the prime goal of all merchants to sell their goods well, since their good or bad fortune depends on this. Much prudence and good judgement is necessary and reason is the guiding principle. The knowledge of how to be a good salesman only comes with much time and experience.

The primary quality which a merchant should have with regard to the sale of his goods is to be a righteous individual. This will assure his salvation and his reputation, the latter being so necessary to traders, who will never make their fortunes without it.

Being a righteous man means being of good faith, and cheating no one. That is, not using false weights and measures which are lighter or heavier than those set down in the ordanances. In dealing with cloth, it means spreading the material out without stretching it in order to give less than full measure. In weighing something, it means not putting one's hand on the scale to make it seem heavier. Finally, it means obeying the law, giving more rather than less of the merchandise, and not representing one type of good as being another.

With regards to the profit which can be made, it is impossible to make rules. If the wares are silk, drapery fabric, serge, or black cloth, whose sale is not affected by changes in fashion; or if they are manufactured in the realm where no import risk is involved; or if they are ordinary, merchants cannot make big profits on them since they are well known.

But on figured and colored cloths whose styles change yearly, and on those which are purely luxury items, considerable profits can be made. What is left over of these items sometimes has to be sold for as much as one-half off. Thus big profits must cancel out these losses, or else merchants would be ruined.

fashion or to the risk of importing them. Everything depends on the judgement and the conduct of the traders.

The apprentice should be careful not to be left with awkward remnants, or remainders. For example, it takes six ells of cloth to make a *deshabillé*., and four to make a suit and coat. If someone bought only one and a half ells, ans awkward remnant would be left, since the unsold material would be useless and thus not sold, entailing a great loss.

One of the prime maxims of merchants is to avoid awkward remnants, since they are impossible to get rid of and eventually become permanent fixtures of the shop.

Since the goods do not belong to him, the apprentice should give no one special prices, merchandise or measures without his master's permission.

The seventh thing which the apprentice must do when selling goods is to be pleasant to the clients. His words should be soft and his efforts to persuade natural and judicious. He must not get accustomed to lying or swearing, nor show annoyance if people rebuff or scorn him. With honesty, he ought to explain that his wares are beautiful and good and that nowhere else could better and cheaper ones be found.

If all his efforts at persuasion fail and the customer leaves without buying anything, the apprentice should not become bad-tempered and nasty in showing him to the door. Instead, he must have a sweet, smiling face, and say that he is sorry not to have been able to sell something to a person for whom he has so much respect, or some other phrase of this type. This politeness often brings people back to the store when they do not find what they are looking for elsewhere; they prefer it because of the kindness and civility which they found there.

This way of acting also results in people's saying good things about those who have treated them well. Thus are young men's reputations established; so that when they set up their own shops they attract customers who respect them; get into the good graces of their masters; sometimes become their partners and marry their daughters, as their virtue and capabilities outweigh their lack of money.

If the apprentice follows faithfully the advice given in this chapter, he will certainly learn to be a retail trader and will manage his affairs well when he strikes out on his own.

19   FROM   *René de Lespinasse (ed.)*
Les Métiers et Corporations
de la Ville de Paris

The Statutes of the Locksmiths' Guild of Paris in Sixty Eight Articles, 12 October 1650. This is the last complete set of rules issued for the locksmiths during the old regime. The rules remained substantially the same until the Revolution. The articles are here summarized, rather than translated directly from the text.

I. A syndic is to be elected by the masters each year. He is the chief administrator of the guild. His term is limited to one year and is not renewable.

II. There are to be four additional elected officers [jurés], two to be elected each year.

III. They must make five inspection visits annually to the shops of masters.

IV. They are given the right to inspect the shops of masters who are set up in the faubourgs and privileged places.

V. They must be ever vigilant in making sure work is properly done.

VI. Reports of infringements of the rule are to be drawn up and given to the royal prosecutor.

VII. Half of any fines collected go to the guild.

X. No master may receive merchandise manufactured outside the city unless it has first been inspected by the officers of the guild.

XI. All locks are to be made by locksmiths and purchased from them in their workshops by members of other trades should they need to do so.

XII. The king promises not to issue any more letters of mastership and revokes those presently in force.

XIII. Masters of the faubourgs and the suburbs must do a masterpiece before they may be considered members of the Parisian guild, but their residence frees them of the requirement to serve terms as apprentice and journeyman.

XIV. No one but locksmiths may sell locks old or new. The officers of the guild have the right of search so that this provision may be enforced.

SOURCE. René de Lespinasse (ed.), *Les Métiers et corporations de la ville de Paris* (Paris: Imprimerie Nationale, 1892), II, pp. 480–493. Translated for this volume by Susan Kaplow.

XV. One must be a born or naturalized Frenchman in order to become a master.

XVII. In order to become a master, one must be Catholic, have been an apprentice and perform a masterpiece. This and the following articles (XVIII–XXI) set down in detail the rules for the performance of the masterpiece.

XXII. The son of a master born after his father had acquired his mastership is not required to perform a masterpiece, but only a much lesser task. Sons born before the acquisition of master's status by their fathers must perform a masterpiece.

XXIII. Five years of consecutive apprenticeship and five years as a journeyman are required for a man to become a master.

XXVI–XXVII. Masters may have only one apprentice at a time, in addition to their sons and one close relation.

XXVIII. A journeyman who wishes to become a master of Paris but who has not done his apprentice for a Parisian master must serve one of them for eight years before becoming eligible for admission to the guild.

XXIX. If such a journeyman marries a master's daughter, his masterpiece is made less difficult.

XXX–XXXV. These articles fix the sums to be paid by aspirants to mastership at various points in their career. Sons and sons-in-law of masters pay less than others.

XXXVII. No apprentice or journeyman may buy or sell merchandise related to the business of locksmithing, under penalty of a 50 livre fine.

XXXVIII. A journeyman may not leave his master's employ without first finishing the work in hand.

XXXIX. Journeymen who are employed on yearly or monthly contracts may not quit before their time is out.

XL. Masters who lure journeymen away from other masters are fined 300 livres and are deprived of "all offices, honors and privileges".

XLI. Apprentices and journeymen are to work only on the master's premises, so as to avoid trade abuses and the manufacture of skeleton keys.

XLII. Widows of masters have a right to continue business in their husband's place, but they may take no apprentices.

XLIII. Journeymen who marry widows of masters will be masters only after eight years service and the execution of a masterpiece.

XLV–XLIX. These articles prescribe ways keys are to be made so as to provide maximum security for locked objects.

L. Scrap metal dealers may not buy or sell goods produced by locksmiths.

LI. No locksmith is to open a lock except in the presence of the master or mistress of the house.

LII. No key is to be made without the lock being in hand; a key may be modeled on another key, only if the locksmith has tested it on the lock to which it belongs.

LIII–LVII. These articles specify in great detail the kinds of goods that artisans other than locksmiths may not produce.

LVII. Parisian mastership is valid throughout the kingdom.

LXVII. No craftsman may use a lock not inspected by the elected officers of the locksmiths' guild.

LXVIII. The affairs of the locksmiths' guild are to be settled by an assembly of masters.

20 FROM   *Émile Coornaert*

Les Compagnonnages en France du Moyen Age à Nos Jours

THE RESOLUTION OF THE DOCTORS OF THE SORBONNE, MARCH 14, 1655

Summary of the impious, sacreligious, and superstitious practices carried on among the journeymen saddlemakers, shoemakers, tailors, cutlers, and hatmakers, when they induct journeymen. . . .

This so called duty of the journeyman consists of three things, to honor God, safeguard the master's property and to maintain the journeymen. But on the contrary these journeymen greatly dishonor God by profaning all the mysteries of our religion and ruining masters by emptying their shops of servants, when one of their cabal complains of having been mistreated. And they ruin themselves by levying fines on one another for the infringement of the rules, which money is used to pay for drinks. Moreover, the *compagnonnage* is of no use to them in obtaining mastership. They have a judicial system among themselves; elect officers . . . keep in touch with similar groups in other cities, have

SOURCE. Emile Coornaert, *Les Compagnonnages en France du noyen age à nos jours* (Paris: Editions Ouvrières, 1966), pp. 350–354. Translated for this volume by Susan Kaplow. Reprinted by permission of the publisher.

a pass word by which they recognize one another and which they keep secret, and form an offensive league against the apprentices [sic— this surely refers to other journeymen] of their trade who are not in their cabal, beat and maltreat them and urge them to join their company. The impieties and sacrileges they commit . . . vary according to the trade. But nonetheless they all have in common the following: first, they make the candidate swear on the Holy Bible that he will tell neither his father nor his mother, his wife nor his children, pastor nor cleric even in the confessional what he is about to do and to see done. And to this end, they choose a tavern which they call the mother, because it is there that they get together as at the home of their common mother, and they hire two comfortable rooms . . . of which one is used for their abominations and the other for the feast. They close the doors and windows carefully so as not to be seen or surprised in any fashion. Secondly, they have the candidate choose a godfather and godmother. They give him a new name such as they consider prop_r: they baptize him derisively and carry out other accursed induction ceremonies peculiar to their several trades, according to the diabolical traditions.

THE SADDLEMAKERS

The journeymen saddlemakers put three coins worth thirty pennies in the Bible; and after the oath has been taken bareheaded on the Scripture and the thirty pieces of silver for which Our Lord was sold, three or four men enter the room. One of them calls for an altar, an altar frontal, ornaments, curtains, a staff, an altar cloth, and other things with which to decorate an altar, an alb, a sash, a stole, a maniple, a chasuble, all the things a priest needs to say Holy Mass, candles, candlesticks, a holy water basin and cruet, a chalice and a saltshaker, salt, a pure and clean loaf of bread; and he is given a cloth that he folds in three to form the three altar cloths with the hems at the bottom, and a cup or glass in place of a chalice, and a penny loaf, and a cross of virgin wax, and the Book, and the thirty pieces of silver, and two lighted candles, and, in place of the cruet, two containers or bottles, one full of wine and the other of water, and salt in a shaker; all these thing having been thus prepared, the room well closed, they all get down on their knees bareheaded. The one who has called for all the things needed for Holy Mass, on his knees, his hands joined before the stool on which all the things are displayed, says to those who wish to become *compagnons*: This bread that you see represents the real body of Our Lord Jesus Christ who was on the three of the cross for our sins; and mumbling some words he says: This wine that you see represents the pure blood of Our Lord which was spilled on the cross for our sins. This said, he takes a piece of bread the size of a pea and puts it into the so called chalice and says: The peace of God be with you; and he puts some salt in the glass and lets three drops of wax drip from the candle, saying: In the name of the Father, the Son and the Holy Ghost. He extinguishes the candle in the so-called chalice. Then he tells the candidates to elect a god-father. All of them on their knees, he baptizes them in a joking manner, profaning the Holy Baptism as he has the Holy Mass, gives some bread to eat to everyone in the room and this adulterated wine to drink. Then they do something else: they take a handkerchief, four glasses full of wine symbolizing the four evangelists, and at the foot of each glass [they put] four small pieces of bread, which have a mean-ing. The cloth on which they get drunk is the shroud of Our Lord, the table is the Holy Sepulchre, the four pillars of the table are the four doctors of the Church; and they do all these and several other heretical things. Huguenots are made members by Catholics and Catholics by Huguenots.

THE SHOEMAKERS

The journeymen shoemakers take bread, wine, salt and water, which they call the four foods, and put them on a table. They place the candidate in front of this table, and they make him swear by his faith, his part of heaven, his God, his chrism and his baptism on these four things. Then they tell him that he must take a new name and be baptized. And he having declared what name he wishes to take, one of the *compagnons* stands behind him and empties a glass of water on his head, saying: I baptize thee in the name of the Father, the Son and the Holy Ghost. The godfather and assistant godfather promise to teach him immediately things having to do with the practice of the group.

THE TAILORS

The journeymen tailors prepare a table in one of the rooms, a table-cloth turned upside down, a saltshaker, a loaf of bread, a tri-stemmed cup half full, three large coins and three needles. After having had the candidate swear on the Scriptures and after he has taken a godfather, they tell him the story of the first three *compagnons*, which is full of impurities, and with which the meaning of the items in the room and on the table have to do. The mystery of the Holy Trinity is profaned several times.

THE CUTLERS

The journeymen cutlers get down on their knees in front of an altar and after having made the candidate swear on the Scriptures, the godfather takes a piece of bread with some salt, which he mixes together and gives to the young man to eat. He has trouble swallowing it, so they give him two or three glasses of wine, all the while affirming that he is now a *compagnon*. A few moments later, they take him into a secluded spot in the country, where they teach him the rights of the admitted member. They make him take off a shoe and they all walk several times round a coat that has been spread upon the ground, so that the unclad foot is on the coat and the other on the ground. They put a napkin with bread and several glasses of wine on the coat, which symbolize the blood of Our Lord, His five wounds, His crown and the nails. The bread symbolizes the body of Jesus; the water, baptism; the fire, the angel; the air symbolizes time; the sky, the throne of God; the earth, the steps to His throne; the wind, the wrath of God; the knife on the table symbolizes the sword that cut off Malchus' ear; the napkin, the holy shroud of Our Lord. They fold the napkin in three and put three stones on it, and say that this symbolizes the three wounds and nails of Our Lord. The handle of the beer stein symbolizes the cross; the two knobs are the two thieves; the part that juts out is the lance used by Longinus to pierce the ribs of the Son of God; the stein is the tower of Babylon, the top and bottom are heaven and earth. The twelve sticks of the wheel that carries the millstone are the twelve apostles; the four elements symbolize the four evangelists. And they question the new *compagnon* about all these things and make him pay fines, each in accordance with his jurisdiction.

THE HATMAKERS

The hatmakers set up a table in the more conspicuous of the two rooms, on which the death and passion of Our Lord are represented.

There is a cross, and a crown made of rolled up napkin placed at the intersection of the two parts of the cross. On the two arms of the cross they put two plates, two candlesticks and two lighted candles, which represent the sun and the moon. The three nails are represented by three knives placed on the two arms and at the bottom of the cross. The lance is represented by a piece of wood; the whips by ropes at the end of a piece of wood; the sponge by a knife and a piece of bread; the tongs by a folded napkin; the lantern by a glass turned upside down; the column to which Our Lord was tied by a saltshaker full of salt; under the shaker they put the equivalent of thirty pieces of silver, for which sum Our Lord was sold; and the salt of the shaker represents the holy chrism. At the foot of the cross they put a basin and a square [tool] with a glass full of wine and water to symbolize the blood and water Our Lord sweated in the Garden of Gethsemani. On the same table they put two glasses, one full of vinegar and one full of gall, a cock and dice, everything that played a part in the Passion. If there is a coffer in the room, it represents Noah's Arc; the buffet, the Tabernacles of Jacob; the bed, the crib in the manger; a chair before the fireplace, the baptismal font; a fagot, the sacrifice of Abraham; and the top of the fireplace represents the pit of hell. The provost plays Pilate and sits in a chair in the most conspicuous place in the room; the lieutenant plays Saint Anne and stands near the provost. The secretary takes the role of Caiaphas and stands in the lowest position. The provost holds in his hand a wand that represents the innocence of Our Lord, with some red color for his blood and some blue color for the black and blue marks of his body. The legs of the table are the four evangelists; the bottom of the table? the Holy Sepulchre; the tablecloth, the Holy Shroud; the cross-piece of the windows, the cross; the two lower panes, the Holy Virgin on one side and Saint John on the other; the two upper panes, when closed, the sun and the moon, when open, the salutation of the angels, because of the brightness that appears. The beams of the room stand for the twelve apostles and the room arch, Our Lord. The candidate is made to take three steps and say at the same time: Honor to God, Honor to the table, Honor to my provost; and stepping up to him, kisses him and says: may it please God that this kiss be not like that of Judas. The provost questions him on the matters described above, and the other *compagnons* are ushered into the room to instruct him. Knocking a first time, they say, *Benedicite*, the second time, *Dominus*, the third, *Consumatum est*; and they are asked: What are you seeking here? They answer: God and the apostles. Finally, to symbolize Our

Lord who was sent from one judge to another, the newly admitted *compagnon* appears before the provost with his legs crossed, unstockinged and in general disarray. He is asked: Whom do you represent? He answers: God forbid that I represent Our Lord. Then he is made to sit down on a chair before the fireplace which represents the font. The godfather and godmother whom he has chosen each take one side of a napkin and tie it around his neck. They put bread and salt in his mouth and, throwing water on him, make him strike three blows on the fireplace and, as a joke, they counterfeit a baptism. He takes a new name and says: I've never eaten anything so salty nor drunk wine so strong. My godfather and godmother have made me strike three blows on the fireplace, by which I recognize that I am an admitted *compagnon*. Then they take a piece of bread from the bed and carry it to the buffet to show how the devil carried Our Lord to the mountain. When a *compagnon* leaves a city, the sack he carries represents Isaac's firewood; when it is on his back, the burden of St. Christopher. The edges of the sack represent Our Lord's legs. They put a sword crosswise on its sheath, and say it is the cross of Saint Andrew. The sheath is the skin of St. Bartholomew. The hiltguard is the guardianship of God. The Chape is Judas' lantern; the point is the lance. Then they seek out a crossroads, hang a glass on a tree to symbolize the death of St. Stephen, and everyone in the group throws a stone at the glass, except the person leaving, who says: My *compagnons*, I am leaving you like the apostles left Our Lord when he sent them to preach the Gospel everywhere. Give me your benediction, and I give you mine.

These journeymen's organizations give rise to several types of disorder. 1) Some of the journeymen fail to keep the oath they take to be loyal to the master, working [only] when they need to and often ruining them by their practices. 2) They injure and persecute the poor boys of the trade who are not in their cabal. 3) They participate in many debaucheries, impurities, drunkeness, etc., etc. and ruin themselves, their wives, and their children through the extraordinary expenditures they make in various meetings of the group, because they prefer to spend the little they have with the *compagnons* than with their family. 4) They profane the days consecrated to the service of God, because some, like the tailors, get together on sundays and go to the tavern where they spend a great part of the day in debauchery. Now, because the said *compagnons* believe that their practices are good and holy, that the oaths they take not to reveal them are just and obligatory, the Doctors [of the

Sorbonne] are asked, for the good of the *compagnons'* consciences, to give their opinion [on these matters] . . . .

We [Doctors of the Sorbonne] . . . think: 1) that there is in these practices sin and sacrilege, impurity and blasphemy against the mysteries of our religion; 2) that the oath they take not to reveal these practices, even at confession, is neither just nor legitimate, nor does it obligate them in any way—on the contrary, they are obliged to accuse themselves of these practices and this oath at confession; 3) in case the evil continues and they cannot remedy it in any other way, they are obliged in conscience to declare these practices to the ecclesiastical judges and even, if necessary, to the secular judges who can remedy them; 4) that the *compagnons* who seek admission in the forms described above cannot use the password that serves to recognize *compagnons* and to engage in their evil practices, without sinning mortally; 5) that the members of these organizations do not have clear consciences so long as they wish to continue the evil practices they ought to renounce; and 6) that non-members may not join without sinning mortally.

21 FROM   *Edmond Pied*
Les Anciens Corps d'Arts et Métiers de Nantes

November 16, 1786. The Royal Police Tribunal of Nantes, upon request of the master weavers, orders:

I. We hereby forbid all journeymen weavers to carry canes, sticks or other arms, either by day or by night, and to form any cabal amongst themselves in order to place one another in work or to quit work. They are forbidden to meet more than three at a time on business concerning the societies called *Devoir* and *Gavotage*,[1] even on the pretext of welcoming a new arrival or for any other reason, under penalty of imprisonment for the first offense, expulsion from the city for one year for a second offense, and perpetual exclusion from mastership for the third offense.

SOURCE. Edmond Pied, compiler, *Les anciens corps d'arts et métiers de Nantes* (Nantes: Imprimerie R. Guist'hau, 1903), IiI, pp. 289–291. Translated for this volume by Susan Kaplow.

[1] I.e., the *compagnonnages*.

II. We likewise forbid all masters, widows, non-resident weavers, tavern keepers and everyone else to shelter the said apprentice [sic] weavers, either for the business of their society of *Devoir* or *Gavotage* or for food and drink when there are more than three of them together, under penalty of fifty livres fine for each offender, to be paid to the guild. Non-payment will make the offender liable to arrest. In addition, masters, widows and non-resident weavers [found guilty] will be obliged to close their shops for a period of six months.

III. It is ordered that the journeymen will be obliged, upon taking up a new job, to show proof to his master of his place of birth, his province and of the city nearest his place of birth and to show the certificate issued him by his last employer.[2]

IV. It is ordered that journeymen workers will be obliged to keep a book in which to insert the several certificates given them by masters for whom they have worked. Masters and non-residents will also keep a register in which they will make a record of the certificates referred to in the previous article. Masters and workers will be expected to show their books upon being asked to do so the first time by officers of justice or by the elected officers [*jurés*] of the guild. Penalties for journeymen will be like those in article I and for masters, like those in article II.

V. It is forbidden to all employers to suborn one another's journeymen either directly or indirectly in order to make them work in their own shop. The penalty will be twenty livres fine, non-payment of which will make the offender liable to arrest. They will also be obliged to fire the said journeymen, who will be made to return to their ex-master under penalty of unemployment.

VI. It is ordered that journeymen who wish to leave their employers either to work elsewhere or to remain unemployed can do so only one week after giving notice and after having finished work they had begun, except in the case of illness or other legitimate cause. Employers may fire journeymen only after eight days notice, in accordance with the statutes of the weavers' guild.

VII. It is ordered that masters, widows, and non-resident employers inform the elected officers of the guild of any law-breaking

---

[2]The practice of issuing certificates to workers when they left a job was both a means of restricting their freedom of movement and of ensuring a stable labor supply.

committed against the dispositions of the present ruling within twenty four hours of their having learned of the same, whether the lawbreaking be done by employers, journeymen or anyone else. In case of silence or dissimulation, the penalties of article II will apply.

VIII. Elected officers of the guild are permitted to inspect establishments whenever they wish in order to discover lawbreaking by employers, journeymen, tavernkeepers and others. They are to make a report to the police commissioners, who will take the action they feel may be warranted.

22 FROM   *E. J. F. Barbier*
Chronique de la Régence et du Règne de Louis XV
ou Journal de Barbier

(July 17, 1725)—On Saturday the fourteenth, a baker of the faubourg Saint-Antoine tried, so they say, to sell for thirty-four sous bread which that morning had cost thirty. The woman to whom this happened caused an uproar and called her neighbors.

The people gathered in fury against the bakers. Soon they numbered eighteen hundred, looted all the houses of the faubourg's bakers from top to bottom, and threw dough and flour into the gutter. Some also profited from the occasion by stealing silver and silverware.

The guards, who are at the city gates during the day, arrived but were pushed back by rocks hurled at them. They had the presence of mind to close the three gates of Saint-Antoine. They sent for a mounted patrol, which forced its way with swords into the midst of the crowd and fired three shots, leading to a general dispersal.

But a terrible tragedy occured. A black musketeer and two officers were on their way into the city, when the musketeer was killed instantly by a shot which struck him in the head. He was a young man of position who had a fourteen or fifteen thousand livre income. He was taken to the city hall and the officers had to restrain the musketeers who wanted to attack the patrol.

Eight of the rebels were arrested and today some of them are being

SOURCE. E. J. F. Barbier, *Chronique de la Régence et du Règne de Louis XV ou Journal de Barbier* (Paris: G. Charpentier et Cie., 1857), I, pp. 350–351, 399–403. Translated for this volume by Susan Kaplow.

hanged in the main street of the faubourg Saint-Antoine. Because of this, a regiment of guards has been called up and since noon has been in control of all the cross streets to prevent the populace from massing to witness the execution. At the same time as the King and Monsieur le Duc, his prime minister, are leaving Paris and preparing to amuse themselves, the people are groaning; for bread is at seven and eight sous the pound and got only with great difficulty.

This is due to the controls put on bread. Farmers are forbidden to bring wheat to the markets and bakers are given only a certain quantity of flour. The kind of bread baked is also regulated: rolls and soft bread are no longer eaten in Paris.

It is true that the weather is horrible. It is continuously raining, perhaps even more-so than before the procession of Saint Geneviève. The results of the procession were only to give enough time to gather in the hay. Nevertheless, the wheat harvest will be plentiful.

There is a passion for bread. Everyone wants more of it than he needs and there are soldiers on guard in the market-places. Measures have even been taken against sedition and the musketeers who were to have gone to Fontainebleau have remained in Paris.

Several mornings signs appeared saying horrible things against the government and against Monsieur le Duc. In a very short period of time we have had to pay [special taxes of three sorts] and bread has been extraordinarily expensive. This is too much all at once not to cause a clamor.

(April, 1724)—The value of money has decreased by one-third this year. Order is being re-established only with great difficulty: this points up the danger of workers' becoming accustomed to earning a lot. It seemed sweet to them to work only three days a week and to have enough to live on for the rest.

One can see how far the factiousness of these lower class individuals goes. In Paris there are perhaps four thousand stocking weavers. When the first devaluation took place, they wanted to have five sous more per pair of stockings, and this the merchants were obliged to give them. At the second devaluation, the merchants wished to reduce the five sous increase. The workers refused to accept this; the merchants lodged a complaint; the workers rebelled.

They threatened to beat up those among them who would work for a lower wage, and they promised one crown [écu] a day to those who would have no work and could not live without it. To do this, they chose a secretary who had a list of the jobless and a treasurer who distributed the maintenance allowance.

These workers lived in the Temple [a privileged area where guild rules did not obtain] They took advantage of the demand for their labor and acted in a seditious manner. A complaint was lodged against them with the controller general and about a dozen were put in prison on a diet of bread and water. This was meant to show the people should not be allowed to get stirred up and also shows how difficult it is to quiet them.

23 FROM   *Louis-Sebastian Mercier*
Tableau de Paris

THE FAUBOURG SAINT-MARCEL

This is the quarter where the poorest, the most restless, and the most undisciplined segment of the Parisian population lives. There is more money in a single house of the faubourg Saint-Honoré[1] than in the entire faubourg Saint-Marcel or Saint-Marceau.

In these dwellings, remote from the central pulse of the city, hide ruined men, misanthropes, alchemists, maniacs, narrow-minded *rentiers*, and also a few studious sages, who are really seeking solitude and wish to live absolutely unknown and apart from the noisy entertainment districts.

No one will ever go to look for them in this remote part of town. If one ventures into this region it is for curiosity's sake: nothing calls you to it; there is not a single monument to be seen. Its people are unrelated to the Parisians, the refined occupants of the area along the Seine.

It was in this quarter that they danced on the coffin of the Deacon Paris, and ate the earth of his tomb until the cemetery was closed:

De par le roi, défense à Dieu
De faire miracle en ce lieu.

SOURCE. Louis-Sebastian Mercier, *Tableau de Paris* (Amsterdam, new edition, enlarged and corrected, 1783), I, pp. 254–258. Translated for this volume by Susan Kaplow.

[1] A district in western Paris which was becoming increasingly the center of bourgeois wealth in the eighteenth century.

[God is forbidden by the King, his Grace,
To make a miracle in this place][2]

Sedition and rebellion have their origins concealed in this hostel of dark poverty.

The houses here have no other clock than the sun; the people are three centuries behind the current state of arts and customs. Every private quarrel becomes public. A woman dissatisfied with her husband pleads her case in the street, brings it to the peoples' court, rounds up all the neighbors, and recites the scandalous confession of *her man*. Every kind of discussion ends in a fist fight. And they are reconciled in the evening only after one of them has had his face covered with scratches.

There, a man holed up in a garret, evades the police and the hundred eyes of their spies, as a tiny insect escapes the most concentrated effort to see him.

An entire family occupies a single room, in which the four walls are bare, the wretched beds lie without covers, and the kitchen utensils are piled up with the chamber pots. All the furniture together is not worth twenty crowns. Every three months the inhabitants, thrown out for owing back rent, must find another hole to live in.

Thus they wander, taking their miserable possessions from refuge to refuge. No shoes are to be seen in their lodgings; the stairs echo only with the sound of wooden clogs. The children are naked and sleep helter-skelter.

On Sunday, the people of this faubourg frequent Vaugirard and its many cabarets. Men must try to forget their troubles, and it is above all they who fill the famous beggars' drawing-room. There men and women, dancing without shoes and swirling without stop, raise so much dust that at the end of an hour one can no longer count them.

A terrible and confused din, a vile odor, everything keeps you from this horribly crowded place. Here, engaged in pleasures suitable for it, the populace drinks a wine as disagreeable as the surroundings.

---

[2] The reference is to the *convulsionnaires*, a sect of Jansenists active particularly between 1728 and 1732. The Deacon Paris was known for his saintly virtues and when he died, his followers claimed that miraculous cures took place at his grave. The jingle quoted by Mercier was found pinned up on the door of the cemetery of St. Médard, which the royal administration had ordered closed.

The faubourg is completely deserted on holidays and Sundays. But when Vaugirard is filled, its people spill over into the Petit-Gentilly, to the Porcherons and to the Courtille.[3] The next day in front of the wine stores lie empty barrels by the dozen. The people drink enough for a week.

This quarter is more wicked, more easily inflamed, more quarrelsome, and more disposed to rebellion than any other. The police are afraid of stirring up the populace, and so handle it gingerly because it is capable of the greatest excesses.

24 FROM   *Friedrich Schulz*
Über Paris und die Pariser

The closer one gets to the center of the city the narrower and, therefore, the dirtier the streets become. Here are the Rues de la Pelleterie, de la Draperie, du Moulin, in which not a single sunbeam penetrates all year long . . . and if one set down a blindfolded foreigner in this network of mainly short, narrow, black, dirty streets and then took the blindfold off and let him guess where he was, it would be impossible for him to know that he was standing in the middle of the finest capital in the world, until he heard the ragpickers and beggarwomen around him addressing one another as Monsieur and Madame.

Here, as in London, women hire sick children and beg with them. The more miserable and frail they are, the more money they cost, because it is assumed that they will bring in more as a result. Many women hire three or four at a time, whom they let hang on to, or carry around with, them, so as to make more obvious how difficult it must be to feed them. Often the children laugh or eat with the most care-free faces, while their carrier assures [her listeners] in tones of deepest misery that they are going to die of starvation. In the Faubourg Saint Antoine, I saw a fight between two beggarwomen which, as a third one

SOURCE. Friedrich Schulz, *Über Paris und die Pariser* (Berlin: bei Friedrich Vieweg dem alteren, 1791), I, pp. 35–37, 52, 63, 206, 372–372. Translated for this volume by Jeffry Kaplow.

[3] Places on the outskirts of the city where wine was sold cheaply at taverns called *guinguettes* because there was no excise tax collected outside the walls.

assured me, had started because one had outbid the other for the hire of a miserable child.

[The watercarriers] are mostly from Auvergne, whence they return to the bosom of their families with a small accumulation of capital after twenty hard, frugal years. They gather together in large groups and rent large or small apartments or stalls in the quarters which they supply with water. Here they sleep at night ten to twenty at a time on straw or mattresses. The oldest man of the group is the advisor and judge, and they hold as strongly to the maintenance of decency and order among themselves as do the Savoyards.[1]

Some [streetporters] wander about the streets of Paris and look through garbage; others go to the promenades and to the livelier places and look for pins, hairpins and similar things [that may have been lost]; others look through the gutters in the middle of the streets to find pieces of iron or brass that may have fallen from horses, harnesses or carriages. So as not to dirty their hands and arms they use a long stick with which they rake through the puddles of water and can detect things as easily as snails can with their antennae. Others gather up in the markets leaves of cabbage, unripe vegetables and bits of straw and get money by selling this to people who keep rabbits, for example. These people never know, when they get up, what they will live on during the day, but comes evening they have eaten and drunk. Only in this city, amongst such a crowd of inhabitants, where everything is sold and must be paid for can people of this sort survive.

I must admit that people pay great attention to bread in Paris and that scarcely a crumb is allowed to go unused. . . . Leftovers that elsewhere are given to domestic animals can be used here for men. In restaurants bread that has lain on the table in crumbs one day is used for the soup the next . . . and in large houses the bread is picked up and sold by the servants or kitchen workers. It sound unusual that crumbs, crusts and cut up pieces of bread should be sold here; but it is true, for I have seen shops full of it in the poor quarters of the city. These breadsellers have a few big houses whose servants deliver leftover bread to them. Thus, one can see in these shops big baskets of bread that varies as to blackness, whiteness, fineness, coarseness and as to whether it is baked with milk or water. The merchant sorts it out methodically and sells it by the pound. It costs only half as much as fresh baked whole loaves. Breadcrumbs are also packed and

[1] Savoyards, i.e., men and boys from Savoie who migrated to Paris to earn a living. They were mainly engaged in running errands, shining shoes and peddling.

are sold to still poorer people for a quarter of the usual price to use in soup.

[Parisians] have always rebelled when bakers have no bread. The recent revolution would not have reached this point had the people had bread. And the people would have forgotten freedom and the hope of freedom if they had been able to forget their stomachs.

25 FROM *Louis-Sebastian Mercier*
Tableau de Paris

THE CHURCH OF SAINT GENEVIÈVE

God forbid that I should scoff at Saint Geneviève, the ancient patroness of the capital! The common people go to rub their sheets and shirts on the saint's reliquary, to ask her to cure them of all kinds of fevers, and consequently drink the dirty water of a supposedly miraculous fountain.

But the municipality, the parliament, and other sovereign courts themselves ask her for rain in periods of drought and for the healing of princess.

When someone is sick, the reliquary is uncovered by degrees, as if to let out more or less of its effectiveness, according to the gravity of the case. When someone is dying, the reliquary is completely exposed.

God forbid that I should scoff at these good people who turn their backs on the holy sacrifice of the mass to prostrate themselves before the shepherdess saint. At this sight, an involuntary smile forms on my lips. But when, on the faces of the faithful, I see the gentle warmth of hope which flares up and burns in their hearts; when I see the feelings of affection with which they are filled; the waiting which consumes them; the confidence which inspires them; then I reproach myself for being unable to share these comforting emotions. Reason and philosophy cannot take the place of these happy and profound illusions.

A cobbler is dying of love for Saint Geneviève, consults her in his

SOURCE. Louis-Sebastian Mercier, *Tableau de Paris* (Amsterdam, new editon, enlarged and corrected, 1783), I, pp. 246–250. Translated for this volume by Susan Kaplow.

troubles, invokes her aid in his pain, calls her name in his afflictions, and feels the transports of the most exalted passion. Like him, I would like to be capable of feeling these ecstatic pleasures in the presence of the reliquary.

I know that nowhere else could I see faces more resplendent before the object of their devotion. I have seen tears fall; I have heard sobs, and sighs which touched me in the depths of my soul. In such moments, I have had respect for this cult, which is suited to the limited intelligence of the masses, and perhaps even more suited to their poverty.

They pray fervently and with all their might. Their hearts melt, soften, and spill over, while the philosopher's soul sometimes remains dry and arid, even though he wishes to ascend to a sublimer and purer cult. . . .

I will return to the foot of the reliquary of Saint Geneviève. I will kneel down among the faithful and respect their belief and their confidence.

I once saw a woman give three shirts to a strong Irishman who, using a long, heavy staff, was able to reach the highly placed saint's reliquary. Having sufficiently rubbed against the sides of the reliquary, the shirts were taken down. But the women asserted that as the middle shirt had not touched the reliquary, it could not have received its miraculous virtues.

She obliged the Irishman to put the middle shirt on the staff again. This time, the rubbing was complete and the woman satisfied. She took it into her head to put her money into a nearby collection-box; the Irishman maintained that it should have been put into the plate and not into the box.

He seemed to be sorry for the trouble which he had taken. The woman took her shirts without bothering about his mutterings and said as she left: they touched the reliquary and I'm proud of it.

Then, curious to read the notes attached to the nearby columns, I went forward and read:

We commend to your prayers a young woman surrounded by seducers and ready to give in.

We commend to your prayers a young man who keeps bad company and stays out all night.

We commend to your prayers a man who is in danger of eternal damnation and who reads philosophical works.

A magnificent church is being built to house this reliquary under a splendid dome. It will cost twelve or fifteen million and perhaps more. What an enormous and useless expenditure, which could have been used for the relief of public misery.

What temple, says the holy book, can be built to Him who has the sky for a cloak and the earth for stepping stones? The curious will go to see the architecture and the populace the saint. They have been working on it for thirty years.

The bones of Descartes lie in the old temple with an epitaph: will they or won't they be taken far away from the reliquary which works miracles? What a mixture, Saint Geneviève and Descartes side by side! They are conversing in the other world: what are they saying about this one? But the humble Descartes has no reliquary.

26 FROM *E. J. F. Barbier*
Chronique de la Régence et du Règne de Louis XV
ou Journal de Barbier

(June 1725)—A miracle occurred in Paris last May during the Corpus Christi procession, and it is so well attested to that even I am forced to believe it happened. There lives in the parish of Sainte-Marguerite in the faubourg Saint-Antoine a forty-five year old woman, the wife of a cabinetmaker. She had been paralyzed for a long time, was unable even to walk about in her room, and also had been bleeding for seven years.

This woman had a profound belief in the Gospel, as we will soon see. She had always wanted to be brought into the street on the day of Corpus Christi in order to kneel before the holy shrine and ask that she be healed. But her confessor, to whom she had spoken of her desire, had a less profound belief than she and had dissuaded her from doing so.

Finally, without speaking of it further, she had herself brought down to the doorway. When the altar came close to her, she crawled on her hands up to it, saying aloud, in the words of the paralytic of the Bible: "My Lord, You can heal me if You so desire."

SOURCE. E. J. F. Barbier, *Chronique de la Régence et du Règne de Louis XV ou Journal de Barbier* (Paris: G. Charpentier et Cie., 1857), I, pp. 390–397. Translated for this volume by Susan Kaplow.

This caused a disturbance. Thinking she was insane, the people even tore her clothes somewhat in their efforts to restrain her. But she immediately stoop up and, in full view of everybody, followed the procession and accompanied the holy shrine to the church like everyone else.

At present, a commission is investigating this occurrence, which is given greater importance by the fact that there are so many Huguenots living in the faubourg Saint-Antoine. All women of the highest social position have been to see this woman or intend to do so. The priest asked her not to attend the lesser Corpus Christi procession as her presence would create too much commotion.

On Saturday June 30th, the parish processions began. These went first to Notre-Dame and then to Saint Geneviève. Motivated either by self-interest in the things of the temporal world, or by their devotion to the Saint, more people than I have ever seen before were in the processions. They were the most pious and solemn I have ever seen heretofore and some of the best bourgeois attended them. The Corpus Christi processions had no one in them by comparison.

There are two big processions. All the poor people of every parish of Paris who are on public relief come to the procession of the Petites-Maisons.[1] They are arranged in groups according to parish, with a verger at their head. The other is the procession of the hospital of the Salpêtrière: this was made up of four to five thousand persons. The sollicitor general [procureur-général] attended both.

The monasteries also had a procession. Saint-Martin-des-Champs has a fine right: that of sprinkling holy water in Paris. I saw a monk who was throwing holy water on the people during the entire march. I have only seen the monks of Saint-Martin-des-Champs do this.

On Thursday [July] the fifth, there took place the procession of the reliquary of Saint Geneviève,[2] one of the most solemn ceremonies in all the kingdom. Only a few drops of rain fell and, as the wind was very strong, the path was dry. The rue Saint-Jacques was filled with people of position; there was a surprisingly big crowd.

The streets were cordoned off. But the archers had only taken their posts at five in the morning and the way was not long. Thus, it was filled with people, so much so that two rows of them had to be removed from either side and sent away up or down the rue Saint-Jacques.

[1] The *Petites Maisons* was a charitable establishment (hospital and residence) for old people.
[2] The Patron saint of Paris.

This could only be accomplished through violence on the part of the foot and mounted guards. It took the procession five hours to pass by and when it arrived at Notre-Dame it was almost two o'clock. It was very badly organized. The procession is headed by an infinite number of Confrères de Jerusalem, who precede the Cordeliers. This makes it very boring, and three-quarters of them should be taken out.

In the morning, the processions go to Notre-Dame, from whence at eight o'clock they leave for Saint Geneviève, taking the rue Galande. The men of Parlament and the other courts arrive separately by another route.

After the high mass, all the processions form an escort for the reliquary, except that of Notre-Dame which goes only as far as Sainte-Geneviève-des-Ardents. There the two reliquaries are bowed as a sign that they are taking leave of one another, and that of Saint-Marcel is returned to Notre-Dame. No one from the courts or the Municipality escorts the saint's reliquary back to the church.

It must be acknowledged that the weather has changed completely since the procession. Of course, the moon changed, but it has always rained despite previous changes in the moon. Nonetheless, the price of bread is considerably higher. Here it still costs four sous the pound.[3]

---

[3]Bread was considered dear when it sold at more than 2 sous 6 deniers or 3 sous a pound.

V   THE PEASANTRY

To write about the French peasantry in the eighteenth century is difficult. First, the concept of a unified peasantry is totally misleading by its very abstraction from the hard realities of village life. There were several kinds of peasants and many different sorts of land tenure. Some of the details of these arrangements are spelled out for us by the celebrated English agronomist Arthur Young in a selection from his *Travels in France*. Young was so fervent a partisan of the new scientific agriculture that he tended to be impatient with any farming that did not conform to his model, hence his strong condemnation of small farms as wasteful and inefficient. It is true that only large proprietors could afford the types of improvements Young desired. In that sense, small farms stopped change. But what was progress? And what was efficiency? In Young's view, progress meant the creation of a national market economy, and efficiency was measured by the amount of produce that could be carried to market—the more the better. While reading Young's account of French agriculture remember that most peasants did not produce primarily for the market, and many had no particular desire to do so.

The size and quality of the land did not alone determine the welfare of the peasant. What mattered was the relationship between the productivity of the land and the burdens it bore. For example, the peasant who had to pay a percentage of his produce to the landlord (the *métayer* or sharecropper) in addition to state taxes and ecclesiastical tithes was less likely to accumulate a surplus, all other things being equal, than the peasant who paid a fixed money rent.

The land-holding peasant, whether proprietor or tenant, needed capital to buy seed, to hire labor (at least for the harvest), and to keep animals. For lack of seed, there might be no crop. For lack of labor, the crop might rot in the fields. For lack of animals, the farmer might have to harness himself, his wife or children to the plow and, worse yet, would have to do without fertilizer. The poor peasant was often caught in a vicious circle of mortgage and debt, but he held desperately onto the little land he possessed because only too often the alternative was to fall into the absolute indigence of the beggar's life.

To this unhappy state tithes, taxes, rents, and the lack of capital, the harrassments of creditors, the low level of argicultural technique all contributed. In addition, the poor peasant had to face the pressure put on the village community by nobles, wealthier peasants, and especially bourgeois of neighboring towns who wished to acquire more land for themselves. This pressure is what Marc Bloch has called the struggle for agrarian individualism. It took the form of attempts to enclose meadows and to divide the common lands on which all village animals were allowed to graze freely. Traditional common rights were also suppressed, so that the peasants could no longer glean the fields after the cutting of the grain and thus obtain the straw used for feed and fuel. Often the use of common rights made the difference between survival and starvation of the poor peasants, particularly for those among them who had only tiny plots of land, as was all too frequently the case. And the totally landless agricultural laborer, the rural proletarian of who Matheiz wrote, was even worse off, if that is possible to imagine.

The documents from Burgundy illustrate the process of disintegration of the village community. First there was enclosure and the end of common rights, then the division of the common lands. Finally, there arrived the bourgeois of neighboring towns who purchase land that the peasants could no longer afford to cultivate. The absentee landlords had no stake in the community. They sought to exploit their holdings for maximum profit, but they neither respected local customs nor played the role of benefactor to local institutions like the Church, which had traditionally been the center of social life. The cohesion of the community suffered, and the future, as the rector of Sornai tells us, looked bleak indeed. Burgundy was atypical of the rest of France only in that it was an extraordinarily rich province, and the immediate effects of these changes *may* have been somewhat less dramatic than elsewhere. In the Auvergne, where the soil was basicly poor and the suffering was endemic, the average peasant had long since been used to life at the subsistence level. The description of that life in the doldrums of winter written by P.-J.-B. Le Grand d'Aussy in 1788 shows how they adapted themselves to this misery. But then they had little choice in the matter.

27 FROM — Arthur Young
Travels During the Years 1787, 1788, and 1789

OF THE TENANTRY, AND SIZE OF FARMS IN FRANCE

There are five circumstances in the occupation of land in France, under which I may include the very numerous notes I took in all the provinces, and which are too voluminous for insertion: 1, the small properties of the peasants; 2, hiring at a money rent, as in England; 3, feudal tenures; 4, monopolizing lands hired at money rent, and re-let to peasants; 5, *métayers*; by which is to be understood, hiring at half or third produce.

I. The small properties of the peasants are found every where, to a degree we have no idea of in England; they are found in every part of the kingdom, even in those provinces where other tenures prevail; but in Quercy, Languedoc, the whole district of the Pyrenées, Béarn, Gascogne, part of Guienne, Alsace, Flanders, and Lorraine, they abound to a greater degree than common. In Flanders, Alsace, on the Garonne, the Béarn, I found many in comfortable circumstances, such as might rather be called small farmers than cottagers, and in Basse Bretagne, many are reputed rich, but in general they are poor and miserable, much arising from the minute division of their little farms among all the children. In Lorraine, and the part of Champagne that joins it, they are quite wretched. I have, more than once, seen division carried to such excess, that a single fruit tree, standing in about ten perch of ground, has constituted a farm, and the local situation of a family decided by the possession.

II. Hiring at money rent is the general practice in Picardy, Artois, part of Flanders, Normandy (except the Pays de Caux), Isle of France, and Pays de Beauce; and I found some in Béarn and about Navarre. Such tenures are found also in most parts of France, scattered among those which are different and predominant; but, upon a moderate estimate, they have not yet made their way through more than a sixth or seventh of the kingdom.

SOURCE. Arthur Young, *Travels During the Years 1787, 1788, and 1789* (Bury St. Edmunds: J. Rackham, 1792), I, pp. 402–417.

III. Feudal tenures—These are fiefs granted by the seigneurs of parishes, under a reservation of fines, quit rents, forfeitures, services, etc. I found them abounding most of Bretagne, Limoufin, Berry, La Marche, etc. where they spread through whole provinces; but they are scattered very much in every part of the kingdom. About Verson, Vatan, etc. in Berry, they complained so heavily of these burthens, that the mode of levying and enforcing them must constitute much of the evil; they are every where much more burthensome than apparent, from the amount which I attribute to that circumstance. Legal adjudications, they assert, are very severe against the tenant, in favour of the seigneur.

IV. Monopoly.—This is commonly practised in various of the provinces where *métaying* is known; men of some substance hire great tracts of land, at a money rent, and re-let it in small divisions to métayers, who pay half the produce. I heard many complaints of it in La Marche, Berry, Poitou, and Angoumois, and it is met with in other provinces; it appears to flow from the difficulties inherent in the métaying system, but is itself a mischievous practice, well known in Ireland, where these middle men are almost banished.

V. *Métayers.*—This is the tenure under which, perhaps, seven-eighths of the lands of France are held; it pervades almost every part of Sologne, Berry, La Marche, Limousin, Anjou, Bourgogne, Bourbon-nais, Nivernais, Auvergne, etc. and is found in Bretagne, Maine, Provence, and all southern counties, etc. In Champagne there are many at *tier franc*, which is the third of the produce, but in general it is half. The landlord commonly finds half the cattle and half the feed; and the métayer labour, implements, and taxes; but in some districts the landlord bears a share of these. In Berry some are at half, some one-third, some one-fourth produce. In Rouffillon the landlord pays half the taxes; and in Guienne, from Auch to Fleuran, many landlords pay all. Near Aguillon, on the Garonne, the métayers furnish half the cattle. Near Falaise, in Normandy, I found métayers, where they should least of all be looked for, on the farms which gentlemen keep in their own hands; the consequence there is, that every gentleman's farm must be precisely the worst cultivated of all the neighbourhood:—this disgraceful circumstance needs no comment. At Nangis, in the Ile of France, I met with an agreement for the landlord to furnish live stock, implements, harness, and taxes; the métayer found labour and his own capitation tax:—the landlord repaired the house and gates; the métayer the windows:—the landlord provided feed the first year; the métayer the last; in the intervening years they supply half and half.

Produce sold for money divided. Butter and cheese used in the métayer's family, to any amount, compounded for at 5s. a cow. In the
Bourbonnais the landlord finds all sorts of live stock, yet the métayer
sells, changes, and buys at his will; the steward keeping an account of
these mutations, for the landlord has half the product of sales, and
pays half the purchases. The tenant carts the landlord's half of the
corn to the barn of the chateau, and comes again to take the straw;
the consequences of this absurd system are striking; land which in
England would let at 10s. pay about 2s 6d. for both land and live stock.

At the first blush, the great disadvantage of the métaying system is
to landlords; but, on a nearer examination, the tenants are found in
the lowest state of poverty, and some of them in misery. At Vatan, in
Berry, I was assured, that the Métayers almost every year borrowed
their bread of the landlord before the harvest came round, yet hardly
worth borrowing, for it was made of rye and barley mixed; I tasted
enough of it to pity sincerely the poor people; but no common person
there eats wheaten bread; with all this misery among the farmers, the
landlord's situation may be estimated by the rents he receives. At
Salbris, in Sologne, for a sheep-walk that feeds 700 sheep, and 200
English acres of other land, paid the landlord, for his half, about 33 l.
sterling; the whole rent, for land and stock too, did not, therefore,
amount to 1s. per head on the sheep! In Limousin, the métayers are
considered as little better than menial servants, removeable at pleasure, and obliged to conform in all things to the will of the landlords;
it is commonly computed that half the tenantry are deeply in debt to
the proprietor, so that he is often obliged to turn them off with the loss
of these debts, in order to save his land from running waste.

In all the modes of occupying land, the great evil is the smallness
of farms. There are large ones in Picardy, the Ile of France, the Pays
de Beauce, Artois, and Normandy; but, in the rest of the kingdom,
such are not general. The division of the farms and population is so
great, that the misery flowing from it is in many places extreme; the
idleness of the people is seen the moment you enter a town on market-
day; the swarms of people are incredible. At Landivisiau, in Bretagne,
I saw a man who walked seven miles to bring two chickens, which
would not sell for 24s. the couple, as he told me himself. At Avranches
men attending each a horse, with a pannier load of sea ooze, not more
than four bushels. Near Issenheim, in Alsace, a rich country, women,
in the midst of harvest, where their labour is nearly as valuable as that
of men, reaping grass by the road side to carry home to their cows.

Three material questions obviously arise; 1st, the inconveniences of métaying, and the advantages of the tenure at a money rent; 2d, the size of farms; 3d, how far small properties are beneficial.

I. *Métayers.* This subject may be easily dispatched; for there is not one word to be said in favour of the practice, and a thousand arguments that might be used against it. The hard plea of necessity can alone be urged in its favour; the poverty of the farmers being so great, that the landlord must stock the farm, or it could not be stocked at all: this is a most cruel burthen to a proprietor, who is thus obliged to run much of the hazard of farming in the most dangerous of all methods, that of trusting his property absolutely in the hands of people who are generally ignorant, many careless, and some undoubtedly wicked. Among some gentlemen I personally knew, I was acquainted with one at Bagnères de Luchon, who was obliged to sell his estate, because he was unable to restock it, the sheep having all died of epidemical distempers; proceeding, doubtless, from the execrable methods of the métayers cramming them into stables as hot as stoves, on reeking dunghills; and then in the common custom of the kingdom, shutting every hole and crack that could let in air.—In this most miserable of all the modes of letting land, after running the hazard of such losses, fatal in many instances, the defrauded landlord receives a contemptible rent;—the farmer is in the lowest state of poverty;—the land is miserably cultivated; and the nation suffers as severely as the parties themselves. It is a curious question how this practice came to be exploded in Picardy, Normandy, and the Ile of France. The wealth of great cities will effect something, but not much; for Bordeaux, Marseilles, and, above all, Lyons and Nantes, have done nothing in this respect; yet they are to be classed among the richest cities in Europe, and far beyond Rouen, Abbeville, Amiens, etc.—And were we to ascribe it to the nearer vicinity of the capital, why has not the same cause established a good husbandry, as well as rents paid in money?—The fact, however, is certain, that those three provinces, with Artois and Flanders, in which we should not be surprized at any variation, as they were conquered from a free country, comparatively speaking, are the only onces in the kingdom where this beneficial practice *generally* prevails. It is found, indeed, in a scattered and irregular manner elsewhere, but not established as in those provinces. That the poverty of the tenantry, which has given rise to this mischievous practice, has arisen from the principles of an arbitrary government, cannot be doubted. Heavy taxes on the farmers, from which the nobility and clergy are exempt; and those taxes levied arbitrarily, at the will of the intendant and his sub-délégués, have been sufficient to impoverish the lower classes. One would naturally have supposed, from the gross abuses and cruelty of this method of taxation, that the object in view were as much to keep the people poor, as to make the King rich. As the taille was professedly levied in proportion to every one's substance, it had the mischievous effect of all *equal* land taxes, when levied even with honesty; for a farmer's profit—his success—his merit, was taxed exactly in proportion to the quantum; a sure method of putting a period to the existence of either profit, success, or merit. The farmers are really poor, or apparently poor, since a rich man will affect poverty to escape the arbitrary rise of a tax, which professes to be in proportion to his power of bearing it: hence poor cattle, poor implements, and poor dung-hills, even on the farms of men who could afford the best. What a ruinous and detestable system, and how surely calculated to stop the current of the wealth of the sovereign, as well as of his people!— What man of common sense and feeling, can lament the fall of a government that conducted itself on such principles? And who can justly condemn the people for their violence, in wresting from the nobility and clergy those privileges and distinctions, which they had used so unworthily, to the depression and ruin of all the inferior classes?[1] These taxes, united with the burthensome and odious feudal rights and impositions of the seigneurs, prevented all investment of capital, which could not be removed at pleasure, from the land: the evil was not so much a general want of capital in the kingdom, as an apprehension of fixing it on land, where it would of necessity be exposed to the rapin of regal and noble harpies; that this was the fact, we find from the case of the rich grazing districts of Normandy, where no want of capital was heard of, yet such lands demand a larger sum to stock than any other; a sum equal to the amplest improvement of the poorest and most difficult soils. Why then should not a proper stock be found on arable as well as on pasture lands? For an obvious reason;— the capital invested in fat oxen and sheep is removeable at a moment's warning; and, being every year renewed, the grazier has an annual opportunity of withdrawing from business; he has consequently a fort of independence, utterly unknown to an arable farmer, who has the least idea of improving his land, or of keeping a proper stock of implements and manure. The knowledge of this circumstance keeps the tyrants in order, and makes them tender in impositions, which being

---

[1] The passage is left as originally written; the people have since shewn in their turn, that the little finger of a democracy is heavier than the whole body of an arbitraty monarch.

evaded, would leave the most valuable land in the kingdom without the means of being rendered productive. In regard to the best means of remedying the evils of métaying, they certainly consists in the proprietor's farming his own lands till improved, and then letting them at a money rent, without the stock; if he can find farmers to hire; but if not, lending the stock at interest. Thus favoured, the farmers would, under a good government and eased of tythes, presently grow rich, and, in all probability, would, for the most part, free themselves from the debt in twenty-five or thirty years; and, with good husbandry, even in a single lease of twenty-one years; but with their present wretched systems of cropping, and deficiency of cattle and sheep, they would be a century effecting it. If a landlord could not, or would not, farm himself, the next method would be, to let live stock and land at a money rent, for twenty-one years, the tenant, at the expiration, paying him in money the original value of the live stock, and subject to all hazards and losses. There can be no doubt but such a system, with a good mode of taxation and freedom from tythes, would enable the métayer in that term to become at least capable of carrying on his business, without any assistance in future from his landlord.

II. *Size of Farms*   I shall begin by asserting, with confidence, that I never saw a single instance of good husbandry on a small farm, except on soils of the greatest fertility. Flanders is always an exception; on that rich, deep, and putrid soil, in the exuberant plain of Alsace, and in the deep and fertile borders of the Garonne, the land is so good, that it must be perversity alone that can contrive very bad husbandry; but on all inferior soils, that is to say, through nine-tenths of the kingdom, and in some instances even on very rich land, as, for instance, in Normandy, the husbandry is execrable. I may further observe, that whenever bad management is found in those rich and well culticated districts, it is sure to be found on small farms. When, therefore, I observed in many *cahiers* of the three orders, a demand to limit the size of farms, and great panegyricks on small ones, I could not but conclude, that the townsmen who drew up those instructions knew nothing of the practice of agriculture, except the vulgar errors which float in every country upon that subject. This inquiry if of so much importance to every nation, that it ought to depend as much as possible on facts, and of course to be handled by those only who practice agriculture as well as understand it. The following question naturally arise. Is it the gross produce of husbandry that should chiefly be considered? Or the greatest produce that can be carried to market?

Or is it the net profit? Should the populousness arising from cultivation be the guide? Or should the ease and happiness of the cultivators be only had in view? These questions might be multiplied, but they are sufficient for unfolding the inquiry. It will probably be found, that no one point is singly to be attended to, but an aggregate of all, in due proportions.

I. The gross produce cannot be alone considered, for this simple reason, that so many hands may be employed to raise the largest, as to afford none for market; in which case there could be no towns, no manufacturers, but merely domestic ones; no army, no navy, no shipping. Such an arrangement, of an equal dispersion of a people over their whole territory, is yet so truly visionary, that it does not demand a moment's attention.

II. The net profit of husbandry cannot possibly be the guide, because the most uncultivated spots may be attended with a greater net profit on the capital employed, than the richest gardens; as a mere warren, sheep-walk, etc.

III. Populousness cannot be a safe guide in the inquiry, because if it be alone attended to, it infallibly destroys itself by excess of misery. There can be no merit in any system that breeds people to starve; food and employment (towns) must, therefore, be in view as well as people.

IV. The ease and happiness of cultivators alone cannot be our guide, because they may be easier and happier in the midst of a howling desert, than in the gardens of Montreuil.

V. I am not absolutely satisfied with the *greatest produce that can be carried to market*, but it comes infinitely nearer to the truth than any of the rest; it includes a considerable gross produce; it implies a great net profit; and indicates, exactly in proportion to its amount, that populousness which is found in towns, and that which ought to depend on manufactures; it secures the ease of the cultivating classes; it enables the farmer to employ much labour, and, what is of more consequence, to pay it well.

This leading proposition, being thus far satisfactorily ascertained, on comparison with the others, we are able to determine that that size of farms is most beneficial, in general, which secures the greatest produce *in the market*; or, in other words, converted into money. Now, in order thus to command a great surplus, above what is consumed by men and their families employed or depending on the cultivation, every species of good husbandry must be exerted. Lands already in culture must be kept improving; great stocks of cattle and sheep supported; every sort of manure that can be procured used plentifully; draining, irrigating, folding, hoeing, marling, claying, liming, inclosing, all must be exerted with activity and vigour:—no scrap of waste land left in a neglected state:—all improved; all pushing forward towards perfection; and the farmer encouraged, by the profit of his undertakings, to invest his savings in fresh exertions, that he may receive that compound interest to practicable for the good farmer. The sized farm that best effects all these works, will certainly carry to market the greatest surplus produce. I have attended, with great care and impartiality, to the result of this inquiry throughout the kingdom; and though in many provinces the husbandry is so infamously bad, as to yield a choice only of evils, yet I may safely assert, that on farms of 300 to 600 acres it is infinitely better than on little ones, and supplies the market with a produce beyond all comparison superior. But by farms I mean always *occupations*, and by no means such as are hired by middle mean to re-let to little métayers. There is nothing strange in the bad husbandry so common on little farms; by which I mean such as are under 100 arpents, and even from 100 to 200; those proportions between the stock and labour, and the land, by which practical men will understand what I mean, are on such farms unfavourable. The man is poor; and no poor farmer can make those exertions that are demanded for good husbandry; and his poverty is necessarily in proportion to the smallness of his farm. The profit of a large farm supports the farmer and his family, and leaves a surplus which may be laid out in improvements; that of a small tract of land will do no more than support the farmer, and leaves nothing for improvements. With the latter the horses are more numerous than with the former, and in a proportion that abridges much of the profit. The division of labour, which in every pursuit of industry gives skill and dispatch, cannot indeed take place on the greatest farms in the degree in which it is found in manufactures; but upon small farms it does not take place at all:— the fame man, by turns, applies to every work of the farm; upon the larger occupation there are ploughmen, threshers, hedgers, shepherds, cow-herds, ox-herds, hog-herds, lime-burners, drainers, and irrigators:—this circumstances is of considerable importance, and decides that every work will be better performed on a large than on a small farm; one of the greatest engines of good husbandry, a sheepfold, is either to be found on a large farm only, or at an expence of labour which *destroys the profit*. It has often been urged, that small farms are greater nurseries of population; in many instances this is the case, and they are often pernicious exactly in that proportion;

prolific in misery; and breeding months without yielding a produce to feed them. In France, population, outstripping the demand, is a public nuisance, and ought to be carefully discouraged; but of this fact, glaring through the whole kingdom, more in another chapter. The farms I should prefer in France would be 250 to 350 acres upon rich soils; and 400 to 600 upon poorer ones.

England has made, upon the whole, a much greater progress in agriculture than any other country in Europe; and great farms have absolutely done the whole: insomuch, that we have not a capital improvement that is ever found on a small one. . . . We have in England brought to perfection the management of inclosing, marling, claying, and every species of manuring. We have made great advances in irrigation; and should, perhaps, have equalled Lombardy, if the liberty of the people would have allowed as ready a trespass on private property. We have carried the breeding of cattle and sheep to a greater perfection, than any country in the world ever yet experienced. We have, in our best managed districts, banished fallows: and, what is the great glory of our island, the best husbandry is found on our poorest soils. Let me demand, of the advocates for small farms, where the little farmer is to be found who will cover his whole farm with marl, at the rate of 100 to 150 tons per acre? who will drain all his land at the expence of two or three pounds an acre? who will pay a heavy price for the manure of towns, and convey it thirty miles by land carriage? who will float his meadows at the expence of 5l. per acre? who, to improve the breed of his sheep, will give 1000 guineas for the *use* of a single ram for a single season? who will give 25 guineas per cow for being covered by a fine bull? who will send across the kingdom to distant provinces for new inplements, and for men to use them? who employ and pay men for residing in provinces, where practices are found which they want to introduce on their farms?—At the very mention of such exertions, common in England, what mind can be so perversely framed as to imagine, for a single moment, that *such things* are to be effected by *little farmers?*—Deduct from agriculture all the practices that have made it flourishing in this island, and you have precisely the management of small farms.

The false ideas, at present so common in France, are the more surprizing, as no language abounds with juster sentiments on many of these questions of political economy than the Franch. There cannot be juster, truer, or more apposite remarks on the advantage of great farms and rich farmers, than in the Encyclopædie. Nor can any one write better on the subject than M. Delegorgue. Artois, he observes, was universally under two crops and a fallow; but changed to a crop every year, by the old customs being abolished. So beneficial an alteration, not common in France, was founded many and expensive experiments, which could be established only by means of the manures gained from large flocks and herds. By whom was this change effected?—by little farmers, who can hardly effect their own support?—assuredly not. He further observes, that some parts of Artois are divided for the sake of a higher rent, and cattle are there sensibly decreased; also, that a country labourer is much happier than a little farmer. And I give him no slight credit for his observation, that little farmers are not able to keep their corn; and that all monopolies are in consequence of them; implying, that great farmers keeping back their corn is beneficial; but monopolies are equally beneficial; and tend as advantageously to remedy the evils that flow from little farmers being in too great a hurry to sell.

But however clearly I may be convinced of the infinite superiority of large farms, and that no country can ever be highly improved, by means of small ones, yet I am very far from recommending any laws or regulations to enforce the union of several. I contend for nothing but freedom; and for the rejection of those absurd and preposterous demands, in some of the French *cahiers*, for laws *against* such an union. And let me add, that little attention should be paid to those writers and politicians, who, under despotic governments, are so strenuous for a great population, as to be blind to much superior objects; who see nothing in the propagation of mankind but the means of increasing soldiers; who admire small farms as the nurseries of slaves—and think it a worthy object of policy to breed men to misery, that they may be enlisted, or starve. Such sentiments may be congenial with the keen atmosphere of German despotism; but that they should find their way into a nation, whose prospects are cheared by the brighter beams of new-born liberty, is a contradiction to that general felicity which ought to flow from freedom. Much too populous to be happy, France should seek the means of feeding the numbers which she hath, instead of breeding more to share a too scanty pittance.

III. *Small Properties* In the preceding observations, I have had rented farms only in view; but there is another sort which abounds in almost every part of France, of which we cannot form an idea from what we see in England—I mean small properties; that is, little farms, belonging to those who cultivate them. The number is so great, that I am inclined to suppose more than one-third of the kingdom occupied by them. Before I travelled, I conceived, that small farms, in property, were very susceptible of good cultivation; and that the occupier of such, having no rent to pay, might be sufficiently at his ease to work improvements, and carry on a vigorous husbandry; but what I have seen in France, has greatly lessened my good opinion of them. In Flanders, I saw excellent husbandry on properties of 30 to 100 acres; but we seldom find here such small patches of property as are common in other provinces. In Alsace, and on the Garonne, that is, on soils of such exuberant fertility as to demand no exertions, some small properties also are well cultivated. In Béarn. I passed through a region of little farmers, whose appearance, neatness, ease, and happiness, charmed me; it was what property alone could, on a small scale, effect; but these were by no means contemptibly small; they are, as I judged by the distance from house to house, from 40 to 80 acres. Except these, and a very few other instances, I saw nothing respectable on small properties, except a most unremitting industry. Indeed, it is necessary to impress on the reader's mind, that though the husbandry I met with, in a great variety of instances on little properties, was as bad as can well be conceived, yet the industry of the possessors was so conspicuous, and so meritorious, that no commendations would be too great for it. It was sufficient to prove, that property in land is, of all others, the most active instigator to severe and incessant labour. And this truth is of such force and extent, that I know no way so sure of carrying tillage to a mountain-top, as by permitting the adjoining villagers to acquire it in property; in fact, we see that, in the mountains of Languedoc, etc. they have conveyed earth in baskets, on their backs, to form soil where nature had denied it. Another circumstance attending small properties, is the increase of population; but what may be advantageous to other countries, may be a misfortune to France.

Having, in this manner, admitted the merit of such small farms in property, I shall, in the next place, state the inconveniences I have observed to result from them in France.

The first and greatest, is the division which universally takes place after the death of the proprietor, commonly amongst all the children, but in some districts amongst the sons only. Forty or fifty acres in property are not incapable of good husbandry; but when divided, twenty acres *must* be ill cultivated: again divided, they become farms of ten acres, of five, of two, and even one; and I have seen some of half, and even a quarter of a rood, with a family as much attached to it, as if it were an hundred acres. The population flowing from this division is, in some cases, great, but it is the multiplication of wretchedness. Couples marry and procreate on the *idea*, not the *reality*, of a maintenance; they increase beyond the demand of towns and manufactures; and the consequence is, distress, and numbers dying of diseases, arising from insufficient nourishment. Hence, therefore, small properties, much divided, prove the greatest source of misery that can be conceived; and this has operated to such an extent and degree in France, that a law undoubtedly ought to be passed, to render all division, below a certain number of arpents, illegal. But what are we, in this view of the subject, drawn from actual and multiplied observations, to think of the men who contend that ten property of land cannot be too much divided? That a country is flourishing in proportion to the equal dispersion of the people over their territory, is the opinion of one celebrated leader[2] in the National Assembly; but his father was of different sentiments; with great good sense and deep reflection he declares, that that culture does not most favour population which employs most hand; "c'est à bien des égards un prejugé de croire, que plus la culture occupe d'hommes plus elle est favourable à la population;" meaning, that the surplus of product carried to market is as favourable to population, by feeding towns, as if eaten on the fields that produced it, *ainsi plus l'industrie & la richesse des entre preneurs de la culture épargne de travail d'hommes, plus la culture fournit à*

---

[2] *De la Monarchie Prussienne*, tom. iv. p. 13. The Count de Mirabeau, in this passage agrees, that great farms, upon a given space of land, will yield the greatest possible production, at the least possible expence; but contends, that there is a multitude of little objects, which escape the great farmer, of much more consequence than saving expences. It is incredible that a man of such decided talents should so utterly mistake the facts that govern a question, to which he has give much attention, at least if we are to judge by his recurring to it so often. Where does he find the fact upon which he builds all his reasoning, that little farmers make larger investments and expences than great farmers? I will not appeal to England, in which the question is determined as soon as named; but I should with to be informed, in what provinces of France the little farmers have their lands as well stocked as great ones? or as well cultivated? M. de Mirabeau completely begs the question, in supposing what is directly contrary to fact, since the advances of the great farms are more considerable, perhaps the double of those of the little one; I am sure it is so in every part of the kingdom in which I have been. But the Count goes on to state how superior the little farms are, because so many more families are found on the land, which is precisely the most powerful argument against them, as that merit admitted, implies at once the annihilation of towns and manufactures being beneficial to a modern state, provided the people be found in the country; a position I have sufficiently answered in the text.

la subsistance d'autre hommes.[3] Another deputy, high in general estimation, and at the head of the committee of finances, asserts, that the greatest possible division of land property is the best. Such gentlemen, with the best intentions, spread opinions, which if fully embraced, would make all France a scene of beggary and wretchedness. Amidst a mass of most useful knowledge, of deep and just reflections, and true political principles, a tendency to similar ideas is found in the reports of the committee of *Mendicité*, in which the multiplication of little properties is considered as a resource against misery. Nothing more is necessary, than to extend such ideas, by supposition to fact, to shew their real tendency. There are 130 millions of acres, and at least 25 millions of people in France. Assign, therefore, to each person, its share of that extent: call it (allowing for rocks, rivers, roads, etc.) five acres each, or 25 acres per family. When, by the first principles of the idea, which is that of encouraging population, the luxury, celibacy, unhealthy employments, prostitution and sterrility of cities are removed, and the plain manners of the country are universally established, every circumstance in nature carries the people to marriage and procreation: a great increase takes place; and the 25 acres gradually, by division, become 20, 15, 12, 8, and so on, perpetually lessening. What, on such a supposition, is to become of the superfluity of people?—You presently arrive at the limit beyond which the earth, cultivate it as you please, will feed no more mouths; yet those simple manners, which instigate to marriage, still continue:—what then is the consequence, but the most dreadful misery imaginable!—You soon would exceed the populousness of China, where the putrid carcasses of dogs, cats, rats, and every species of filth and vermin, are fought with avidity, to sustain the life of wretches who were born only to be starved. Such are the infallible effects of carrying into execution a too minute division of landed property. No country upon earth is cursed with so bad a government as that would be, which aimed seriously at such a division; so ruinous is that population, which arises from principles pure and virtuous in their origin, but leads directly to the extremes of human misery!— Great cities have been called the graves of the human species; if they

[3] "It is in many ways a prejudice to believe that the more men are occupied in agriculture, the more agriculture is favorable [to the growth of] population..."— "Thus the more the industriousness and the wealth of agricultural entrepreneurs spares manpower, the more does agriculture furnish for the maintenance of other men." The persons referred to here are Mirabeau, father and son.

conduct easily to the grave, they become the best *euthanasia* of too much populousness. They are more apt to prevent increase than to destroy, which is precisely the effect wanted in such a country as France, where the division of property has unhappily nursed up a population, which she cannot feed; what, therefore, would be the misery of cities and towns supported their numbers, and left the whole surplus of the country regorging in the cottages?—This is too much the cafe for the happiness of the kingdom, as we see in a thousand circumstances, and particularly in the distress arising from the least failure in the crops; such a deficiency, as ie England passes almost without notice, in France is attended with dreadful cala-mities.

There cannot be a more pleasing spectacle, or better framed to call into animation the sympathies of our nature, than that of a family living on a little property, which their industry cultivates, and perhaps created: it is this object, so touching to the best feelings of the human bosom, that has certainly made many writers indiscriminate advocates for small properties. If the industry of towns and manufactures were active enough to demand the surplus of all this population as fast as it arose, the advantages of the system would be clear; but France knows, by sad experience, that such a surplus is not demanded at present; what, therefore, would the consequence be of bringing a fresh one to market, while the old one remains on hand? It is idle to cite the ex-ample of America, where an immensity of fertile land lies open to every one who will accept it; and where population is valuable to an unex-ampled degree, as we see in the price of their labour; but what com-parison, between such a country and France, where the competition for employment is so great, arising from too great a populousness, that the price of labour is 76 per cent. below that of its more flourish-ing neighbour?—But, in considering this interesting subject, I shall recur, as I have done on so many other occasions, to the example of England. In this kingdom, small properties are exceedingly rare; in great numbers of our counties, there are scarcely any such thing to be found: our labouring poor are justly emulous of being the proprietors of their cottages, and of that scrap of land, a few perches, which form the garden; but they seldom think of buying land enough to employ themselves; and, as in France, of offering prices so much beyond the value, as to ensure the acquisition; a man that has two or three hundred pounds with us, does not buy a little field, but stocks a farm: now, as our labouring poor are incomparably more at their ease, and in every respect happier than those of France, does it not appear to follow, by fair conclusion, the small properties are by no means necessary for the welfare of the lower classes in the country? in every part of England, in which I have been, there is no comparison between the ease of a day-labourer and of a very little farmer; we have no people that work so hard, and fare so ill, as the latter. Why then should this minute division be considered as so advantageous in France, while we in England feel the benefit of a system directly contrary? There are several reasons for this; the manufactures of France, compared with those of England, are not nearly so considerable respectively, in proportion to the population of the two kingdoms. Nor does the agriculture of France, which is carried on either by farmers or métayers, afford any employment comparable to that which English culture yields. Country gentlemen, in France, do not employ probably the hundredth part of the labourers that are employed by country gentlemen in England, who have always some works of ornamental gardening or farming going on, which gives bread to many people. An object, more important, is, that the prices of provisions are as dear in France as in England, while those of labour are 76 per cent. lower. We have another proof, if any were wanted, how much too great the population of that kingdom is. The English labourer, who commands steadily eight, nine, or ten shillings a week, by working for a farmer, hazards much when he labours land for himself; and this fact is so strong, that the most industrious and hard labouring of our poor peasants, are not those who keep their little gardens in the best order and cultivation; but such, on the contrary, as make inferior earnings, that mark something of debility. By means of these, and various other causes, the poor countrymen in England find a much more regular employment by day labour than those of France, who, having no resource in working for others, are obliged to work for themselves, or starve. And when gentlemen find them in this situation, no wonder they readily expatiate on the advantages of small properties being to such families the only resource that offers. But, in fact, the very height of operose culture upon such, and what appears perfection to a vulgar eye, can arise only from the misery of half employed people. The dearness of labour, very common in such a country, is no proof against this observation. No labour is so wretchedly performed, and so dear, as that of hired hands accustomed much to labour for themselves; there is a disgust, and a listlessness that cannot escape an intelligent observer; and nothing but real distress will drive such little proprietors to work at all for others; so that I have seen, in the operosely cultivated parts of France, labour comparatively dear, and ill performed, amidst swarms of half idle people. And here I should remark, the circumstance seen to so strange a degree in almost all the markets of France, that swarms of people regularly lose one day in a week, for objects that clearly shew the little value time is of to these small farmers. Can any thing be apparently so absurd, as a strong hearty man walking some miles, and losing a day's work, which ought to be worth 15 to 20 *s*, in order to sell a dozen of eggs, or a chicken, the value of which would not equal the labor of conveying it, *were the people usefully employed?* This ought to convince us, that these small occupations are a real loss of labour; and that people are fed upon them, whose time is worth little or nothing.

There are many practices in French husbandry, that are apparently of considerable merit, yet cannot be recommended to other countries. I have seen them, in a part of Flanders, mattocking up every corner of a field where the plough could not come; and, in the south of France, the peasant makes a common practice of mattocking up whole fields.[4] In many parts of the kingdom all the land is digged. In the mountains of the Vivarais, terraces are built by walling, and the earth carried to them in baskets. Such practices and a thousand other similar, spring absolutely from the extreme division of landed property, having nursed up a population beyond the power of industry to support; and ought to be considered as a proof of a real evil in the vitals of the state. The man who unhappily has existence in a country where there is no employment for him, will, if he has the property of a scrap of land, work for two-pence a day upon it; he will work for half a farthing; and, if he has an ardour of industry, for nothing, as thousands do in France. If he does not perform some business, upon his little farm, he thinks he does nothing; in such a situation, he will pick straws— he will take up a stone here and lay it there: he will carry earth in a basket to the top of a mountain; he will walk ten miles to sell an egg. Is it not obvious to the reader, that such practices existing, and, if tolerably directed, producing an effect well calculated to command admiration from an extreme of culture, are in reality no more analogous to a well constituted country, if I may venture the expression, than would the most preposterous practices to be fancied. You might as well go a step further in population, and hold up, with M. de Poivre, the example of the Chinese, as worthy of European imitation.

Upon the whole, one must be inclined to think, that small properties are carried much too far in France; that a most miserable population

---

[4] A mattock is a hoe. Hence, to mattock, is to turn up the land with this instrument.

has been created by them, which ought to have had no existence; that their division should be restrained by express laws, at least till the demand for hands is equal to the production; that the system of great farms regularly employing, and well paying a numerous peasantry by day labour, is infinitely more advantageous to the nation, and to the poor themselves, than the multiplication of small properties; in fine, it is obvious, that all measures which prevent the establishment of large farms, and increasing wealthy farmers, such as restrictions or bars to inclosures, the existence of rights of commonage, and the least favour to little proprietors in levying of the land taxes, are ruinous to agriculture, and ought to be deprecated, as a system destructive of the public welfare.

28   FROM   *P. de Saint Jacob*

Documents Relatifs à la Communauté Villageoise en Bourgogne du Milieu du XVIIe Siècle à la Révolution

ROYAL EDICT CONCERNING ENCLOSURES IN BURGUNDY, AUGUST, 1770

Louis by the grace of God, King of France and Navarre, to all persons now and in the future, Greetings. The Estates General of our Duchy of Burgundy has asked us to be so good as to authorize the inhabitants of that province to enclose the land which belongs to them or which they cultivate. The report that we have had drawn up concerning the state of agriculture in Burgundy and the special laws relative thereto has put us in a position to realize how important it may be to enact a law that is so advantageous to agriculture. For these reasons and others, on the advice of our Council and with our full knowledge, power and royal authority, we have ordered the following perpetual and irrevocable Edict:

SOURCE. P. de Saint Jacob, compiler, *Documents relatifs à la communauté villageoise en Bourgogne du milieu du XVIIe siècle à la révolution* (Dijon: Imprimerie Bernigaud et Privat, 1962), pp. 87–88, 112–115, 149–154. Translated for this volume by Susan Kaplow.

Article I.—We hereby allow all proprietors, cultivators, farmers and all our subjects of the Province of Burgundy to enclose land, meadows, fields and, in general, all other holdings belonging to them or cultivated by them in as great a quantity as they may think proper, either through the use of ditches, or quickest or dead hedges, or in any other manner.

II. —Land that is enclosed will no longer be subject in future and so long as it remains enclosed to the exercise of common rights nor open for the pasturage of animals other than those belonging to the owner or farmer of the land. To this effect, we hereby repeal all contrary laws, customs and usages.

III. —Nonetheless, enclosure of land may not take place in such a way as to interfere with the passage of animals on their way to such pasture lands as many remain open to them. Nor shall an enclosure interfere with the passage of plows and carts needed for the cultivation of the land and the gathering of the harvest. To this effect, every proprietor must allow free passage on his land, if [by traditional custom] he is subject thereto or cannot enclose his land without interfering with the said passage.

IV. —The enclosure of holdings will be paid for by their proprietors in common, if they consent to do so; but if neighboring proprietors refuse to participate, the site of the enclosure will be taken from the land to be enclosed.

V. —For six months from the day of the registration of the present Edict, deeds drawn for the exchange of parcels of land of less than ten arpents will be exempt from transfer taxes and other royal and seigneurial dues, with the exception of the registration tax which will remain set at ten sous whatever the value of the parcels in question may be. The parcels will, however, remain subject to the same land taxes, seigneurial dues, and tithes as before the exchange was effected. . . .

Signed: Louis

EDICT ON THE DIVISION OF COMMON LANDS,
JANUARY, 1774

Louis by the grace of God, King of France and Navarre, to all persons now and in the future, Greetings. The numerous encouragements that we have given to agriculture at various times ought to have proven how important it appears to us to be. The successes they have had have convinced us that agriculture alone is the source of the real riches of our kingdom. The land clearings carried out in execution of our Declaration of 13 August 1766 having restored to production and developed land which had produced nothing until then, we have directed our attention to another kind of landed property, which is uncultivated and much greater in extent. The common pasturages given to village communities by kings, our predecessors, or by individual seigneurs have become arid and sterile through lack of cultivation. They seem to us to be worthy of our care, because of the possibility of drawing from them the greatest advantage for our people; and we were thinking of means of securing for them all the advantages which their donors had intended, when the Estates General of the province of Burgundy . . . in the third article of a list they presented to us last year, and the syndics and consuls of the third estate of Bugey and Gex in deliberations taken on this subject asked us for permission to divide them among all the inhabitants of the said provinces. We have noted with an especial satisfaction the zeal and eagerness of the said Estates, syndics and consuls to procure the greatest good for the said provinces and to have them share in the aid we are giving to agriculture. Consequently, wishing to give our subjects of the province of Burgundy . . . and of Bugey and Gex new proofs of our paternal benevolence for them, we have found it advisable to defer on this point to the joint supplications of the said Estates General of Burgundy and of the said syndics and consuls of the third estate of Bugey and Gex. For these reasons and other considerations prompting us to do so, on the advice of our Council and with out full knowledge, power and royal authority, we have ordered the following perpetual and irrevocable Edict.

I. —We hereby allow all the communities of our province of Burgundy, the counties of Maconnais, Auxerrois and Barsur-Seine and of Bugey and Gex who desire to do so to divide among all existing households, without distinction as to widows, spinsters and bachelors who keep separate homes and pay taxes, and the seigneur's share reserved, when there is reason to do so, all or only part of the arable, meadows, swamps, waste-land or uncleared land belonging to them in common, but not including woods, in the manner hereafter to be explained. To this effect, we hereby revoke all contrary laws, usages, orders and regulations.

II. —The deliberations of the communities will take place in a general assembly convoked in the usual manner. They will be received and directed by a royal notary, who will keep a record in his archives and will give a copy of the deliberations to the inhabitants. The record will contain any opposition to the division of the land formulated by one or more inhabitants, and the causes of this opposition. The deliberations will be signed by at least two thirds of those participating and who know how to sign. They will then be signed by the Intendant, after which they will be presented to the Court of Parlement at Paris or Dijon or to the *comités superieurs* in whose jurisdiction the communities are situated, to be ratified and registered without cost.

III. —The shares given to each individual inhabitant will be indivisible, inalienable and not subject to seizure by creditors of the owner with the exception of their produce, which the said creditors may have assigned to them [by court order]. But the provisions of the present article may in no way infringe the rights of seigneurs or of any other individual possessed of well established real land rights on the common lands that are to be divided.

IV. —No individual not domiciled in the village may have a share and no inhabitant may possess more than one. The surplus shares or those which become vacant will be farmed out by the mayor and councilmen for three years at a time for a money rent for the benefit of the community. During the said interval inhabitants not provided for may claim their shares, those who have lived longest in the village to be taken care of first; in which case, the rent of the first year of the lease will belong to the community and the rent for the remaining years will be paid by the farmer to the inhabitants who have become owners of the land. The latter may not cancel the leases granted by the community.

V. —All the shares will be hereditary in the direct line only and those which fall to a collateral relation or become vacant, in whatever manner, will be granted by the community to those among the non-possessing inhabitants who have been married the longest, and the fruits of the year will belong to the estate of the last possessor.

VI. —The land may be willed to one of a man's children who has a household in the community, but without prejudice to the right of the widow to the usufruct during her lifetime. For lack of a will in favor of one of the children, the entire holding will belong to the eldest of the children settled in the community.

VII. —To avoid all arguments to which the variety of rights belonging to the seigneurs *haut justiciers* may give rise, we wish the said seigneurs or all other persons who can prove the concession of rights attached to the *Haute Justice*[1] to be allowed, in the case where *Triage*[2] may take place, to take for himself one third of the common lands whose division had been asked and decided upon by the communities, the parcels to be chosen by lot or by negociation. After the said one third levy, the seigneurs may not demand any due or payment of whatever kind other than the right of administering justice on the other two thirds divided among the members of the community. However, the seigneurs can not be forced to settle for one third of the common lands to be divided and thus to give up dues and payments which may belong to him on the said communal lands [i.e., the seigneur may prohibit the division from taking place, if it is to his advantage to do so.

VIII. —Common lands thus divided, including the portion due the seigneur, will enjoy the privileges and exemptions enumerated in articles V and VI of our Declaration of 13 August 1766 in favor of persons clearing uncultivated lands.

IX. —In so far as Bugey is concerned, all domiciled inhabitants of the communities, even those who pay only the capitation tax, will participate in the division of communal land; we also intend to guarantee all rights and privileges in Bugey which municipal laws may have established concerning the division of the said land between the inhabitants and the seigneur.

X. —We wish all disputes which may arise in regard to the division of communal lands to be in the first instance within the jurisdiction of the judge exercising the *Haute Justice*. No dispute may be adjudicated until the *procureur fiscal* [in a feudal court the equivalent of the attorney general in a royal tribunal] shall have considered the case and drawn up his recommendations.

REPORT OF LASSUS, VICAR OF SORNAI, ON THE CONDITION OF HIS CHURCH AND VESTRY, SEPTEMPER 4, 1787

The time is no more when the inhabitants of Sornai rivalled all the inhabitants of the surrounding parishes in wealth and comfort. In

---

[1]Haute Justice refers to the right to hold a seigneurial court, a powerful weapon used by lords to keep their peasants in line.

[2]When a seigneur could prove that it was he (or his predecessor) who had given the use of the common land to the peasant community, he could demand the return of one third of the parcel. This was called *triage* (selection) and always took place when the commons were divided. The seigneur often received more than his legitimate share.

those days, the Church reflected the opulence of those who came to it
for religious ceremonies; each person, according to his means, tried
to outdo the other in contributing to its maintenance and adornment.
The painting on the altar of the Virgin, a very clean chasuble, an alb,
a banner are the remaining monuments attesting to the zeal and fortune of the last wealthy inhabitants who, with good grace, supple-
mented the small revenue of the Church.

The Thiellands, the Vincents, the Boulys, the Lécuelles, the Carrés,
the Cailleres, the Florets, the Galands, the Juliens were not only ones
who did themselves the honor of furnishing the Church the necessary
and proper things which it could not procure for itself. They are no
more. Their names have passed on to descendants who are now but
feeble agriculturalists, impotent farmers, miserable cottagers, and
some even bad landless laborers. Their land has fallen into the hands
of the bourgeois of Louhans. These are today the absentee landlords
who bother little about the upkeep of a Church that is not their own.

Revolutions, which sometimes cause the decline of states, do not
always remove the hope of a better future. But is there any hope left
for Sornai? Will it be to poor people like those of Sornai that the
bourgeois will sell their lands? If circumstances force them to it, will
they not always find buyers in Louhans where they live? Thus I am
correct in supposing that the initial decrease in the resources of the
Church is due to the cessation of former generosity and to the inability
[to contribute] of the present inhabitants.

The second follows from the first. Sunday and holiday collections
no longer produced what they once did, far from it. This is too obvious
to require elaboration.

The third cause of the decrease in Church revenues comes from the
prohibition on burial in the Church. There used to be no wealthy or
comfortable people who were not so buried, and even those who were
less well off were at pains to acquire for the dead person the same
honor which his ancestors had had. In a parish of more than seven
hundred communicants rich as I have stated, the prohibition of tombs
in the Church has, in truth, caused a considerable deficit.

The fourth cause of decrease is truly the result of a change in the
road. Formerly, it passed right by the Church. People who had some
interest in it could not pass by without feeling themselves solicited,
as it were, to be generous. People sometimes passed by at the time of
the parochial mass, and the example of the inhabitants sometimes
produced an adventitious collection. Today the collections account
for no more than thirty livres a year.

The Church is thus reduced, so to speak, to fifteen livres of revenues very badly farmed out and badly paid, and thirty livres of lease revenue which also comes in but slowly, in all forty five livres. I said *so to speak*, because the marriage bans at five sous each also produce about ten livres, but not everyone pays. Here then are the revenues of the Church of Sornai:

Contractual income:	45 livres	
Marriage Bans:	10 livres	
Collections: very uncertain:	about 30 livres	
I estimate the possible total at:	45 livres.	

Now the charges and expenditures of the Church are much greater than the income. Thus everything is falling into ruin, nothing is repaired for lack of the means to do so. Nothing is maintained. In the end, taxes are necessary which crush the people and turn them against the man who sollicits them. This is ordinarily and always the vicar, who ought to enjoy the confidence and friendship of everyone, if he is to produce results in his work.

[He then lists in detail all the expenditures necessary to repair the Church and finds that the money to do so is nowhere to be found in the parish. He suggests:]

Easy means to endow the Church and fabric of Sornai without burdening the people:

The inhabitants of Sornai possess common lands of about fourteen of fifteen hundred *journaux*,[3] part of which was formerly wooded and is now all in brush; the remainder produces only brambles or moss or a very short grass. Besides that, they have as grazing land a very vast meadow and two smaller pieces of land near the village, not to mention those found in the outlying hamlets. To ask for one of these small pieces of land near the village to be made into an enclosed meadow for the benefit of the vestry would be to deprive them of grazing land for their geese and sheep, but two thirds of their commons would be more than sufficient for the grazing of all kinds of livestock. So as not to turn them against me I would even not ask for the third that might be taken from it for the Church without interfering with the pasturing of the animals, no matter what they say against it. In a word, even

---

[3] A *journal* (pl., *journaux*) was a land measure supposed to correspond to the amount of land a man could plow in one day's labour. It is impossible to give a modern equivalent.

a hundred *journaux*, which is neither the tenth nor the twelfth of the total but is in any case quite a lot, with that much land one might make the Church rich. And this without touching a single piece of the present pasturage such as it has been used over the last ten years. One might endow the Church without bothering anyone, except those who, having been unable to keep their property, are happy to see poverty spread everywhere as well as in their own home.

Several individuals in the last ten years have with temerity usurped pieces of common lands adjoining their holdings or their home, others have taken what they could, some have taken one *journal*, some two, according to their capacity to cultivate them. These lands belonging to the community do not bring it any profit. The usurpers have cleared them and made good use of them. It would be very much a pity now to put back into fallow for the purpose of grazing land which produces good grain, the more so as the present grazing land is more than sufficient to the needs of the community. However, by virtue of a communal decision of 1783 approved by the Intendant [Amelot] these usurpers are being sued to force them to return this land. Four have already been ordered to do so, and four others have been convoked to undergo the same fate, as successively they all will be. I think it would be a very good idea to give to the vestry the usufruct of these lands cleared and already cultivated, rather than to restore them to their state of uselessness in which they were formerly. The vestry would be authorized to lease them out to the highest bidder with the preference given to those who have taken the trouble to clear them, if they agree to the same conditions as the others. Thus the communal property would be of profit to the community, since it is the community which constitutes and forms the vestry of Sornai.

The obstinacy with which any individual usurper might speak against and resist, without any plausible reason, this plan that I propose would only end up by causing him to be compared to those insatiable men who deprive themselves of food in order to store up and admire their treasures endlessly.

Here is the most practical plan for endowing the poor vestry of Sornai. Or else, we will be obliged to pay the taxes that we like so little. One of the four beams supporting the belltower in the form of a pillar is so rotten that already the Subdelegate, who has property in Sornai, has joined me in asking the inhabitants to have this column changed promptly, to repair the roof, the windows and the floor. They contended themselves with opening their eyes wide and allowing their mouths to hang open. Such is the peasant; he knows what is necessary, but his lack of means makes him fearful, he decides on nothing and does not let himself be persuaded to do anything. I certify that I believe I have said only what is true and possible.

Sornai 4 September 1787   Lassus, vicar

The vicar of Savigni succeeded in getting some of the common lands for his church only on the occasion of the division of the common lands last year, when the division was made into as many parts as was thought proper and useful. Division cannot take place for diverse reasons in Sornai, but the example of Savigni proves that portions of common lands are sometimes given to churches that need them; and Sornai is surely in this position, whereas, on the contrary, Savigni already enjoyed a decent income.

29 FROM *Pierre Jean Baptiste Le Grand d'Aussy*
Voyage d'Auvergne

The rest that the work animals enjoy in the time of the snows is shared by the peasant. The year, for him, is divided into two semesters, one of complete inactivity, another of hard labor. And even the working half of the year is, by the nature of the produce gathered in the mountain districts, limited to three periods of activity: the sowing of oats in May, after the snow has thawed; the hay cutting season towards the end of July or the beginning of August; and finally the grain harvest at the end of August or towards the beginning of September. This last period is really a time of fatigue for the farmer. Because it is necessary to reseed before the return of the snows, he has not a moment to lose. The harvest is no sooner cut and gathered in then he begins to plow. A part of his night is spent threshing the wheat that is needed for seeding. At dawn, he goes to plant it; and then he continues to plow and so on, until all the seed is sown. At this time he gets scarcely even a few hours of sleep; but as soon as the earth is covered with snow, his idleness begins; and it lasts six months, without any work

SOURCE. Pierre Jean Baptiste Le Grand d'Aussy, *Voyage d'Auvergne* (Paris: Eugene Onfroy, 1788), pp. 280–287. Translated for this volume by Susan Kaplow.

whatsoever, and during this time he leaves his home only to go to church or to carry his grain to the neighboring markets, if he needs to sell some.

The scarcity and dearness of firewood in the mountains ought to make the peasant suffer greatly during the winter. He has found a means not to have heat, by living with his livestock. Ordinarily his habitat is divided into three parts: on the right, the stable; on the left, the barn; in the middle, the house: all of the parts constituting a single building with doors separating one part from another. When the cold begins to make itself felt, the peasants leave the house; and the entire family moves into the stable which, from this moment on, becomes their winter quarters.

The form of the stables is an elongated square topped off by an attic in which hay and other dry forrage for the cattle is kept. It has two dormer windows, without panes, to provide some light; and two doors, of which one opens on to the outside and one leads to the house. But to make the stables warmer and at the same time to have a larger attic, they are built very low. The animals occupy the two sides, right and left; the family's beds are at the back in the warmest place, so that to get there one has to pass through the double rank of animals. These beds, for the rest, are a kind of pine boxes placed in a fixed position end to end against the wall and covered with straw. The poor have only a blanket in addition to the straw. Those who are better off add to it a kind of mattress or large sack filled with oat husks. This sack is called a field mattress; because it is in the fields that the oats that provide the husks of which they are made grow. Only the rich have featherbeds; it is a luxury of which people are very jealous. Thus a girl who, on getting married, brings a dowry to her husband never fails to have inserted into the marriage contract a clause to the effect that the husband will give her a feather mattress for her bed and not a field mattress.

The life a family leads in its stable is very strange. They rise at eight or nine o'clock. The father then goes with his male children and his hired hands, if there are any, to take care of the animals and to change their litter. The wife, during this time, goes into the house with her daughters. They light a faggot of briar and make a soup. A meal is eaten but as quickly as possible, so as not to get cold; then they run back to take refuge in the stable. In the evening, at five o'clock, there is soup once again; and then a new retreat until dinner [i.e., the morning meal] the next day.

On Sundays and holidays, a bit of salt pork is put into the soup;

on other days it is made with butter and often even with pure salt. However, at the tables of the well off peasantry, a little milk and cheese is served. The bread is made of rye; flour and bran are mixed together, which makes it heavy, sticky and black. Add to this the fact that since bread is baked only twice during the winter on account of the shortage of wood, it gets hard as ship's rations. As to beverages, there is only water or a kind of small milk that flows from cheese when it is put under the press.

It is the women who are burdened with all the details of the housework. It is they who milk the cows, make butter and cheese. Thus they get up earlier and go to bed later than the men. When new snow falls and covers the road to the pump, one of them takes on the job of clearing a new path. Sunk into the snow sometimes up to the waist, she goes and comes several times in a row and finally establishes a route for her friends. A man would think himself dishonored if he went to find water himself; and certainly he would be the laughing stock of the village. These mountain yokels have a deep contempt and despotic disdain for women, which is proper to all savages and semi-barbarous peoples. They look on them as slaves, destined to do all the work they consider servile and which they disdain. In their view, their only occupation is to feed the cattle, unless need forces them to tresh grain and to go to the neighboring markets. Outside of that, their lives are made up, like those of the savages, of profound inactivity and idleness.

It is very seldom, however, that a family spends the winter alone and isolated in its stable. Ordinarily several households get together; and if one of them has a stable that is larger or warmer than the others, that is where the day is spent and the assembly is held. In the morning, as soon as the soup has been eaten, everyone comes running; they sit down on benches arranged in a circle; and I don't have to tell you what the time is used for. They chat, laugh and complain about taxes; they tell stories about the girls of the neighborhood. They say bad things about the priest, the landlord and everyone else who isn't there. At five o'clock they break up to go eat their soup; then they come back to chat a little while longer. And then they go back home to sleep.

Women being very little involved in all these male gossip sessions and running the risk of spending a whole day without talking, they have arranged things so that they too may have a turn. And in good faith, this is fair enough. First, when the discussion gets going again after supper, they doze a little to gather their strength. No sooner have the men withdrawn than, having become mistresses of the terrain, they go to, and God knows how they make up for lost time! During this time the master of the stable sleeps in his box, but since, after all, it wouldn't be right that he give the women a place to talk *and* pay the cost of their pleasures as well, the women have a special lamp for their night gossipings, the cost of whose oil is shared among them. This money is earned by spinning which, happily, doesn't stop them from talking. But alas, all good things must come to an end; towards midnight or one o'clock they must say good night—and it is over until the next evening.

In certain villages, whose priests have trained the inhabitants to a greater devotion, the custom has been established that the households who get together in the same stable perform their religious duties in common. In the morning, after everyone has arrived, a rosary is said. During the day, canticles are sung; and finally in the evening, before the men go to bed, prayers are said. All this devotion doesn't stop the swearing and the off color stories from beginning again a moment later—but at least religion interrupts them for a few moments.

In other places pious exercises do not take place among stablemates. Each person prays God when and how it pleases him to do so; but the greater part of the evenings are spent in dancing. The man in the group who is considered to be the best musician stands up and sings. Those of the women who don't dance accompany him with their sharp voices; and everyone else, yelling with joy, jumps and capers heavily, while the oxen chew their cud to the cadenced noises of the wooden shoes.

30 FROM   *F. Y. Besnard*
                      Souvenirs d'un Nonagenaire

When I arrived in Nouans [A village in the department of the Sarthe], I noted with admiration that the land was generally divided into fields of about 6 or 7 arpents each, surrounded by hedges and ditches, planted with fruit trees, especially with apple trees which were then in flower. Moreover, the fields were covered with different kinds of crops: cereals, clover, hemp, vetch, beans, etc.

SOURCE. F. Y. Besnard, *Souvenirs d'un Nonagenaire* (Paris: Librairie H. Champion, 1880), I, pp. 80–81, 296–304. Translated for this volume by Susan Kaplow.

At that time, I knew nothing about the growing of clover which, by itself, covered almost as much of the land as wheat. Oxen, cows and horses grazed in it with the grass as high as their stomachs; or mowers cut it down for fodder. Next to this, very fine hemp covered the greatest part of the fallow. Finally, I marveled at the fact that no plot of ground was uncultivated.

Here is what I shortly discovered according to the enquiries I hurried to make and to an analysis of the harvests of my estate. Wheat yielded 9 to 1, barley 16, oats 20, hemp 800 pounds of flax, and clover four thousands per arpent.[1]

Aside from the harvest of clover cut down while green or used to pasture the animals . . . the farmers set aside for seed a more or less considerable amount of the second cutting. And this harvest varied, as circumstances were more or less favorable to its growth, from 100 to 150 pounds per arpent.

As soon as Dom Gallais, accompanied by the curate and the sacristan, had left for Le Mans, I began my visits to the people of the parish. I went into all their houses and profited from the occassion to examine their barns, their work animals, etc.

I saw to my chagrin that the farmers were poorly housed. They had only one large front room, which served as kitchen and refectory for masters and servants, and bedroom for the family; and another bedroom behind this first one, sometimes a second room serving as a living-room. I saw also that the stables, sheds, and pens were narrow, low, and unhygienic; that the yards were not walled and that they usually held the drinking trough and the manure ditch.

But I saw with pleasure that the room which contained the oven and which served as bakery, laundry, and dairy, was detached; and also that livestock was generally plentiful and just as fat as it should be.

Thus I observed that farms of 40 arpents usually had 6 oxen, 6 milch cows, 6 heifers, 6 bulls from 1 to 3 years old, 2 brood mares, 60 to 70 sheep of average size, 4 or 5 pigs of which 1 was a sow. In addition, their barnyards held, besides chickens and ducks in sufficient quantity, a large flock of geese. In the three bigger farms, the livestock was proportionally greater in number.

I also saw with pleasure that all the arable land was cultivated with the plow. Because of this, small farmers or owners of five, six or seven arpents got together in groups of two to form a team of two

[1]An *arpent* varied in size from five-sixths of an acre to one and a quarter acres.

horses. Those who had smaller amounts of land made arragements
with neighboring farmers who did their plowing and transported
their fertilizer and harvest at a price fixed in money and working days.

All the gardens were fairly well furnished with vegetable plants,
and most had some trees which gave edible fruits, and even some
flowers such as roses, carnations, lilies, and gillyflowers.

The food of the inhabitants, even the poorest, was substantial
and plentiful. The bread, into which went no more than one part
barley for two parts of wheat, was very good, and the cider, more
or less weakened with water, was nowhere lacking. At dinner and
supper, soup was followed by a meat, egg, or vegetable dish. For
breakfast and collation, they had two dishes, butter and cheese,
and often a third one of uncooked, cooked, or dried fruits, apples,
nuts, etc.[2]

The whole dish was put on a table covered with a cloth and
each person, supplied with a plate, a spoon and a knife, took whatever he wanted. Following custom, they only began to eat when
everyone who should have been there had arrived; this prolonged
the time of the meal indefinitely.

On the farms, the consumption—especially of back fat, eggs,
butter, and cider—was enormous. I soon had the proof of this. As
to meat, a piece of salted pork weighing 200 to 240 pounds with the
leftovers of my table, the produce of three well-fed cows, and 2 or 3
dozen chickens would not have been sufficient for my three servants
if not for the tubs of butter and baskets of eggs I received so frequently as gifts. This explained to me why the farmers then sent
neither of these commodities to market. As to cider, about 25 barrels
of it were drunk and about one and one-half of wine, distributed
during periods of extraordinary work.

Although several of these farmers were extremely well-off, none of
them had wine delivered to their houses by the barrel. Their habit
was to get as much as they needed from the tavern, where they sent
their bottles in baskets of 10 and 12 to be filled . . . only to repeat
the process when this small supply was exhausted. Even the notary
followed this practice.

[2]Besnard is evidently speaking of a highly privileged area. Peasants' food was
in the main limited to the traditional soup made of milk and water, a little fat, a
few vegetables and thickened with bread. Meat was consumed rarely, and even eggs
and cheese were not plentiful. Wine or cider (depending on the region) drunk by
peasants was of poor quality and generally cut with water to make the supply last
longer.

Both men and women went to the tavern. In fact, it was there that all business was transacted, from the sale of a couple of oxen to requests for a day-laborer, a tailor, a dressmaker or a seamstress, and the payment of even the smallest salaries.

The most highly regarded wines in the canton and in the upper Maine were those of Château-du-Loir. In the lower Maine, these were considered light wines and those of the Anjou were preferred.

On Sundays and holidays, the town's three taverns were always full from the end of the first mass until evening. Nevertheless, people did not stay in them during the church services, which attracted about as many of the faithful to Vespers as to high and low mass. Red wine was not consumed there at this time. There were only three or four drunkards—the notary, a farm owner, a peasant, and an artisan. This type of intemperance, even on the part of a churchman, did not shock anyone.

The garments of men and women, although made of cloth called de façons—that is, woolen or cotton material spun and made on the spot—were clean and comfortable. What greatly surprised me when I first arrived was that the clothing of the rich and of the farmers was indistinguishable from that of simple day-laborers or even of poor people. This was also true of shoes and of underwear; the difference only became apparent on holidays.

Neither the ones nor the others had that tanned or sun-burned complexion so common in the upper region of the Anjou and among inhabitants of the countryside. It is true that the women were rarely employed in hard work out-of-doors, and never in grain threshing, for example. The women did not breast feed the infants, who were bottle-fed with cows' milk.

Unless it was rainy, women went to church and to market with nothing else on their heads than their usual head-gear.

Such was the gentleness of manner of men and women alike that words and, with all the more reason, acts of brutality were extremely rare within families, between neighbors, and even in relationship to animals.

Although during the thirteen years which I spent in that commune I was often called to forestall court cases or to reconcile parties, I never was summoned to break-up a brawl.

[At Les Alleuds, in the Maine-et-Loire] the workers employed in threshing the grain from the estates were not fed and received as their only salary every seventh bushel of the different types of grains. They were obliged to cut the grain, to form it into sheaths, to pile it up in the barn or into stacks, to winnow it and to transport it to the lofts set aside for it, and furthermore to hoe the said grain on spring days yearly assigned them. They were given a place and the wood necessary to prepare their food.

The workers employed in threshing the grain of the *dîme* received only every thirteenth bushel, as they did about half the work of the others.

Farmhands received wages for the year, which began for them on the feast day of Saint John the Baptist [June 24] and ended on the same day of the following year. The first plowhand, since he exercised some authority over the others, got 84 to 90 francs; the three carters got 54 to 66 francs; the three goads got 30 to 36 francs; and the stable boy working in the garden got 60 to 66 francs.

The wages of the female servants were the following: for those working as domestics, 36 to 42 francs; and for the other two, 24 to 33 francs. In addition, each of the latter was given one or two pair of wooden clogs and one or two measures of cloth.[3]

Their food was very meagre. In the afternoon and evening, and sometimes even in the morning as during the sowing, mowing, and grape-harvesting seasons, soup was given them. For breakfast and for collation, they ate bread with butter or cheese, which the head female servant distributed to each one on the point of her knife, or with fruits such as apples or nuts, of which she also gave an assigned number to each one.

For the afternoon and evening meal, she also determined each person's portion, which she gave him on a plate or which she distributed when it was lard or some other meat. Their drink was a light wine obtained from grape or apple marc or from sorb-apples dried in the oven; and during times of heavy labor, a few glasses of wine.

---

[3] For the significance of these wage figures, cf. the observations of Gaillard d'Allières for the same area, in Part One.

VI THE CAHIERS DE DOLÉANCES

When it was decided in the fall of 1788 to call the Estates General into session for the first time in 175 years, an elaborate electoral system was set up to designate the deputies of each Order. There was much conflict over these procedures, and, indeed, the procedures were so contrived that they all guaranteed that the Third Estate would be represented by rich and/or prestigious bourgeois (as it turned out, many of them were lawyers) rather than by peasants and artisans. But each voting assembly, from the smallest village right up to the *bailliage* that finally chose the deputies to the Estates General, had a right to draw up a list of complaints called a *cahier de doléances*.

Not every one of these was laid before the Estates General. Rather, the demands they contained were sifted through by a committee at the *bailliage* meeting, whose task it was to integrate them into the final *cahier* to be sent to Versailles. The committees were generally staffed by a majority of urban bourgeois who tended to disregard demands that were not to their advantage or simply did not concern them. Thus, to look only at the *cahiers* of the *bailliages* is to neglect a whole range of grievances formulated at the lower levels not only of the electoral system but of society itself.

The *cahiers* of the Third Estate presented here have been chosen with a view toward avoiding this distortion. This said, it is true that there was a remarkable degree of unanimity on certain issues, such as the need to divide the tax burden more equitably, to create favorable conditions for the development of internal and external trade, and to establish the powers of a periodically convened Estates General. Even many nobles, such as those of the *bailliage* of Nemours, were willing to take on their share of taxes and to adopt the principle of the equal protection of the laws, so that the freedom of the individual might be guaranteed.

Notice the differences of emphasis within the *cahiers* of the Third Estate; they contain the germs of later disagreements. These would come to the fore very early in the Revolution, once the principal demands concerning the right of the National Assembly to exist had been won through the action of Parisian shopkeepers and artisans on July 12–14, 1789. The peasants of St. Georges, the artisans of Rouen, and the bourgeois of Versailles (whose *cahier* is the perfect expression of the revolutionary program of 1789, even in its very hesitations) might be able to agree on a minimal program, but they soon parted company when it came to a question of going beyond equality before the law to establish some sort of social equality— or should one say social democracy. Their views on the economic basis of society were radically opposed to one another. For example, bourgeois could not agree with artisans on the latter's demands for the limitation of grain exports and the prohibition of machinery. The only unity possible within the Third Estate was that imposed by the necessities of the struggle against monarchy and nobility. Once victories won made this unity less urgent, the coalition was quick to break up. Not even the threat of foreign invasion and war was ever capable of restoring it entirely.

31 FROM *Cahier des Pouvoirs et Instructions du Député de l'Ordre de la Noblesse du Bailliage de Nemours*

THE CAHIER OF THE NOBILITY OF THE BAILLIAGE OF NEMOURS

I. The wish of the nobility of the bailliage of Nemours is that places in the meeting hall of the Estates General be occupied without distinction of province or deputation, so as to avoid anything that may be interpreted as conferring preeminence on province or another.

II. That the president of the order of the nobility in the Estates General be freely elected by and in his order, without distinction of province or rank.

III. That the persons of the members of the Estates General be declared inviolable and that in any case they may not answer for what they had said or done in the Estates General to any but the Estates General.

IV. That the wish of the order of the nobility of the bailliage of Nemours is that the vote be by order.

V. But in case that voting by order is absolutely rejected by the Estates General and the deputy of the bailliage sees that further resistance to voting by head would be useless, he will ask that voting by head be done in the separate chambers of each order and not in a general assembly of the three orders together.

That the Estates General decide how many votes beyond half will constitute a majority.

Vote by head can never be allowed in matters concerning only one of the three orders.

VI. That the nobility of the bailliage wishes to declare at the outset to the Estates General that its intention is that taxes be generally and equally divided among individuals of the three orders.

And that, always wishing to set an example of the most entire obedience to the laws of the realm, the nobility asks that criminal and civil laws which ought to protect all citizens equally may apply to everyone, without regard to rank or birth.

SOURCE. *Cahier des pouvoirs et instructions du député de l'ordre de la noblesse du bailliage de Nemours*, 16 March 1789 (Nemours, 1789). Translated for this volume by Susan Kaplow.

VII. That the nation having come together in the assembly of the Estates General, it regains all its rights and, as a consequence, all taxes presently established must be declared null and void, as not having been voted by the nation, which alone has the power to do so.

IX. That the wish of the nobility of the bailliage is that individual freedoms be guaranteed to every Frenchman, before any other matters are dealt with; that under the rubric of freedom be included the right to go and come, to live anywhere he pleases in and outside the realm, without need of any authorization; and that it be up to the Estates General to determine the cases when it may be necessary to infringe this freedom, in so far as it concerns leaving the kingdom.

X. That any person held or arrested in any manner whatsoever be given over, within the time set by the Estates General, to his usual [i.e., local] judges, and that it be ordered that he be questioned within twenty four hours and a decision on his detention be taken in the shortest possible time.

XI. That bail be allowed, except in the case where the prisoner is accused of a crime which may lead to corporal punishment.

XII. That any person, other than ordinary judges and police officers, who signs a detention order may be brought up before the competent judges not only to be condemned to pay damages, but also to be corporally punished, in the manner ordered by the Estates General.

XIII. That freedom of the press be granted, with such exceptions as may be determined by the Estates General.

XIV. That the most absolute respect for letters sent by post be likewise ordered, and that the Estates General find the best means to insure their safety.

XV. That agriculture, industry, arts and commerce enjoy the greatest freedom and be delivered from the monopoly resulting from excessive privileges.

XVI. That all property rights be inviolable, and that no individual be deprived of property except for the single reason of the public interest and that, in such a case, he be indemnified without delay in a manner determined by the Estates General.

XVII. That the Estates General be constituted according to just proportions among the three orders, and that legislative power be given them in its entirety. Therefore in order to have full force, this legislative power need only be sanctioned by the royal assent.

XVIII. That the high courts, whose task it is to be the depository of the laws, may not submit the laws to any examination, nor modify any of their clauses.

XIX. That in the Estates General after the current one, the first two orders be combined in a single chamber, on the express condition that this chamber . . . be composed in the proportion of one member of the clergy to two members of the nobility. That any matter dealt with in the first or second chambers may be proposed, rejected or accepted in the other, so that the free consent of the two separate chambers be necessary to give force of law to anything deliberated upon by them.

XXII. That in case of war, a change of reign or a regency, the Estate's General be assembled within six weeks.

XXIII. That the Estates General meet every two years, dating from the end of the first assembly.

XXIV. That each Estates General be newly elected.

XXV. That in case the Estates General meet for more than one year at a time and circumstances make necessary a continuation of deliberations, the Estates General should be nonetheless dissolved and new elections held . . .

XXVI. That no tax be granted except for a limited time, at most for two years, dating from the day of the dissolution of the Estates General. That the said taxes may neither be assessed nor collected after that date, the collectors being liable to prosecution as extortionists.

XXVII. That the Estates General establish no body, of whatever name, to represent and/or work in its name.

XXIX. That ministers be accountable to the Estates General for the use of monies granted them, and responsible to the said Estates General for their conduct in everything having to do with the laws of the kingdom.

XXX. That reform of the civil and criminal code be taken up, so as to speed up the process of justice, to lessen its cost, to ensure open hearings, and to bring the courts closer to the parties who may be called before them.

XXXI. That there may be no denial of justice in any case or to any person.

XXXIV. That the Estates General go on to no further deliberation until the law passed by them on matters already considered is promulgated [i.e., given the Royal sanction].

XXXV. That the constitution being thus determined, the deputies ask the minister of finance for a statement of the present situation of the finances of the kingdom.

XXXVI. That this statement be discussed, accepted or changed, as it will please the Estates General to decide.

XXXVII. [The debt to be consolidated by the nation.]

XXXIX. That no loan, in any form whatsoever, no paper money, no office or commission of any kind whatsoever be created or established except by the will and consent of the nation assembled.

XLI. That agricultural day laborers and the poorest inhabitants be exempt, if possible, from all taxes.

Matters Relating to the Provinces

XLII. That it be stipulated that only that portion of the taxes will leave the provinces as cannot be used there.

XLIII. That consequently there be created and established throughout the realm administrative assemblies made up of members freely elected in each province, charged with assessing and collecting the taxes of each province. These assemblies are to have authority in all administrative matters.

XLIV. That the said administrative assemblies be considered only as being delegated by the provinces, and that they be accountable to the Estates General only.

XLVI. That a reform of the vexatious and abusive militia system, whose effects are so prejudicial to agriculture, be undertaken.

XLVII. That because the *capitaineries*[1] form a jurisdiction which is foreign to the laws of the kingdom, being a manifest violation of the sacred right of property, and because many people use these usurped rights in a cruel and oppressive manner, the Estates General should decide upon their entire destruction as soon as possible. That kings and princes be limited in this regard to the simple right to hunt on the lands and seignories of their domains.

XLVIII. That the regime of the *eaux et forêts*[2] being illegal, abusive and vexatious, it be absolutely abolished, and that the execution of such rules as may seem necessary to the Estates General be entrusted to the administrative assemblies.

XLIX. That the Estates General find a way to commute the

[1] A *capitainerie* was a jurisdiction having authority over hunting in royal game preserves. This demand is equivalent to calling for freedom to hunt as one wishes.

[2] The *Eaux et Forêts* was the court that dealt with all matters concerning the forests and waterways of the royal domain.

banalité dues[3] into an equivalent one that will be less onerous to the people.

L. That the abolition of the *franc fief* due be asked of the Estates General.[4]

LI. That means be found to abolish the disastrous salt tax.

LII. That there be only a single set of weights and measures in the markets of each province.

Matters Relating to the Bailliage

LIII. That the *aides*, more burdensome in the bailliage of Nemours than anywhere else in the realm, be reduced, until the Estates General have decided on means of replacing them.

LV. The wish of the nobility of the bailliage of Nemours is that the Estates General increase the number of educational establishments for both sexes throughout the kingdom, and particularly in this bailliage, which is totally lacking in them. That means be found to improve the schools of surgery, midwifery and of veterinary medecine.

Matters Relating to the Nobility

LVII. The wish of the nobility of the bailliage of Nemours is that they share with all citizens the payment of state taxes, but that this engagement may in no way compromise their property rights, both real and honorific.

LVIII. That obstacles which prevent the third estate from occupying all positions and offices be abolished.

LIX. That no employment or profession result in the loss of nobility.

LX. That in future no right of reversion be granted.[5]

---

[3] The *banalités*, feudal dues paid to the seigneur for the grinding of flour, the baking of bread and the pressing of grapes. The use of the lord's mill, oven or press was often obligatory.

[4] The *franc fief* was a tax levied on noble land bought by a commoner. By virtue of the Declaration of 1771, it was equivalent to one year's revenue in each twenty years.

[5] The right of reversion (*Survivance*) is the right to succeed to a person's office after his death.

LXI. That no venal office henceforth confer either the privileges of nobility or hereditary nobility, and that this distinction may be awarded only for long and useful service rendered to the state, verified by the vote of the provinces.

LXII. That new research directed against usurpers of titles of nobility be ordered, and that a permanent tribunal be established to check on the proofs and to judge any disputes relating to them.

LXIII. The wish of the nobility of the bailliage of Nemours is that it may keep the right belonging to the order to march to the defense of the state, should the feudal host be convoked.

LXIV. That measures soon be taken to suppress and reimburse military venal offices.

LXV. That no person occupying an office or employment at Court may be a deputy to the Estates General.

LXVI. That military employments and political positions no longer be regarded as offices of the Court, distributed to a few families who possess them as a matter of hereditary right, so to speak.

Matters Relating to the Clergy

LXVIII. The desire of the nobility of the bailliage of Nemours is that every bishop and abbot be obliged to reside in his diocese or abbey and that they not be permitted to have another residence of any sort in any city of the kingdom.

LXIX. That clergymen who have no particular functions to fulfil but who enjoy benefices be placed in the dioceses to busy themselves with matters suited to their station.

LXX. That the Estates General seek means to limit the extent of ecclesiastical fortunes and to distribute them in a better fashion.

LXXI. That vicars be given an increase in income, which will permit them to perform the charitable acts to which their station calls them.

LXXIII. That the clergy be subject to the taxes borne by the nobility and the rest of the nation.

LXXIV. That the Estates General decide what to do about the debts of the clergy.

LXXV. That the clergy may debate on taxes only in national assemblies [rather than in local or regional ones.]

LXXVI. The nobility of the bailliage of Nemours thus ends its [lists of] powers and instructions and expresses to its deputies its .

most absolute wish that the Estate General grant no tax before decisions have been taken on all their demands and laws passed by them have received the sanction of the royal assent.

32 FROM *Cahiers de Doléances du Tiers Etat du Bailliage de Rouen*

THE CAHIER OF THE HATTERS AND FURRIERS OF ROUEN

The assembled guild having honored me with its votes to be the bearer of its complaints, I have tried, in so far as I have been capable of so doing, to give the greatest clarity to the formulation of the diverse demands of the said guild, of which I am happy to be a member, on account of the intelligence that presides over its affairs and is its principal rule of conduct in all the burdens that it must bear in order to satisfy the monarch's will. If, for lack of knowledge that is not given to all craftsmen, I have not expressed their ideas in terms proper to each complaint, I ask the indulgence of the respectable assembly in whose presence I will state them. The great and suitable terms are a body of knowledge that an artisan does not always have the possibility of acquiring . . . Because the necessity of seeking the general good, which is the motive for all our meetings, has not limited the complaints of each guild to matters that concern it exclusively, I have undertaken to speak of all matters that may tend to the salvation of those classes of men most burdened by taxes and of the poorest class, and to put an end to the growing misfortune resulting from present circumstances. . . .

1. The land tax has been adopted and unanimously recommended to constitute a single tax and to be applied to all landed property in both city and country, whether it belong to the clergy, nobility or third estate, without distinction. This tax seems all the more legal, as the social contract in a great kingdom devoted to its king recognizes and allows to exist only one family, the eldest member [i.e., the nobility] of which owes to his younger brothers the example of paying taxes for the maintenance of the state.

SOURCE. M. Bouloiseau, ed., *Cahiers de Doléances du Tiers Etat du Bailliage de Rouen* (Paris: Presses Universitaires de France, 1957), I, pp. 106–116. Translated for this volume by Susan Kaplow.

2. That trade ought to be exempt from all customs duties within France is another of our demands. One notes with sorrow that this large family, since I have used the term because I believe it does honor to humanity, has to pay enormous taxes on goods entering and leaving the conquered provinces like French Flanders and Brittany in general and others when it wishes to clothe itself, despite the fact that all are governed by a common monarch. The kind of inquisition that makes minute exactness of declarations so necessary is so vexations that everything may be lost on account of the least little mistake, for the omission of an object of little consequence found when a bundle is inspected, and all is seized by a company which is both judge and party in its own case. Therefore in order to give trade all the liberty it needs to flourish once again, we ask the abolition of customs within the kingdom.

3. The abolition of the *aides* [excise taxes on alcoholic beverages] is similarly asked, because of all the harassment they involve. A man cannot give his poverty stricken neighbor a bottle of wine that has paid enormous taxes when it entered the district. There is an example of an unfortunate man who wanted to help another and was arrested on account of one bottle of wine, and a third party, charitably and by arrangement after many discussions, paid 536 livres to relieve him of the penalty imposed by the rulebook. We ask then that this tax be abolished throughout the kingdom so that, as a result, it will be possible to help the unfortunate and to get from the vintner all drinks whatsoever with the addition only of the cost of transportation. This will avoid the abuse of permits at the gates or barriers which . . . put the unfortunate teamster, who thought he was making a living by hauling a barrel of drink, at the mercy of the tax farmer who confiscates the cart, the horses and moreover has the driver fined.

4. The salt tax is revolting both in essence and on account of its unfortunate results. Salt, which is manna from heaven, that the [tax] farmer pays one sou and sixpence for is sold at 13 sous the pound. Does this sale price bear any proportion to its true price? Does transportation cost explain this increase? It costs hardly a penny a pound. Is the storage cost responsible, for salt must stay a while before it acquires the proper degree of goodness so that it may be consumed? But this also costs only a penny a pound. Is it the interest charges on money advanced to buy the salt? Open your eyes, and you will see that a barrel of salt that cost the tax farmer 360 to 400 livres produces 3000 livres, which constitutes an enormous and revolting profit. What is the result of the tax farmer's attempt to safeguard this pre-

cious item? He hires clerks, chosen in truth from the class of unfortunates, who wage open war against men as unfortunate as they who are trying to lighten the burden of their misery by lessening the price of this product, which is of the greatest necessity to them. . . . The tax farmers have abused the king into ordering every individual to purchase a certain quantity of salt. This rigorous law condemns a man to pay a fine if he has not paid his salt tax and to be hanged if he is found in possession of a handful of salt which is considered to be illegal, because it was not bought of the tax farmers.

5. The punishment of the galleys makes mankind cry out in pain. We ask that this no longer be the punishment of those unfortunates whom necessity has led to defraud the taxes, whom need has often forced to rebel against the clerks who do not earn enough not to engage in vexatious actions, clerks who are so little thought of by their superiors that often they are disavowed when a protective hand takes up the defense of the unfortunate who has committed fraud, or when the smuggler is himself a man whose means lead him to plead against the tax farmers, so that his voice may reach the king's ear. We ask, then, that this punishment no longer be applied except to those men who bear a mark branded on them by the courts as a result of being convicted of theft or pocket picking.

6. We also demand the freedom of the tobacco trade throughout the realm. The present system is subject to all the bad features mentioned above in regard to salt. . . .

7. The unfortunate year we have just lived through is the object of another demand, and is the one which this respectable assembly ought to put before the monarch as being the most dangerous scourge in a kingdom made to provide law and order for everyone and to be an example to everyone by its wise laws and wise means of preventing all disastrous happenings: that is, the permission to export grain.

It is said that grain is lacking in all the provinces of the kingdom; this comes either from bad weather or from the abuses that result from it. Let us see if the bad weather is as bad as it is said to be. Interested persons have succeeded in striking terror in men's hearts and have brought about a progressive rise in the price of a foodstuff of the utmost necessity because, if we look closely at the events, the disastrous hailstorm that ravaged diverse districts was not of such an extent as to cover an area great enough to cause the resultant misfortune to have effect almost everywhere in the kingdom. And if one wishes to consider that the affected part of the realm is in the proportion of a dot to the size of this page, can one imagine that the immense portion that was free of this scourge cannot provide for the needs of so small an area. In that case it would be necessary to admit that the total of all land cultivated is insufficient to feed all the subjects of the kingdom.

The present evil has, then, a cause which is much more terrible, because it is revolting to mankind; it is that a number of persons interested in raising prices are men who store grain for export and then force a rise great enough to satisfy their avidity for the gold that flows from it. There are examples of immense storehouses of grain covered with mites. But they wait for prices to rise before putting it up for sale and they sell only at the last extremity, when its quality is deteriorating, which often leads to illnesses of unknown origin. . . .

In a kingdom such as France, it is necessary to have supplies for two years in order to avoid accidents, and the law ought to provide for this. . . . And in the future exportation of grain should be permitted only when the *mine* of grain weighing between 145 and 150 pounds costs not more than twelve livres. At that price all men can live, from the property-owning peasant to the poorest workers.

8. A matter difficult to deal with concerns bankruptcies. The law has been laid down to me on this item, but happily it has only to do with fraudulent bankruptcies, for so many citizens have been troubled and are daily troubled by the [poor] state of trade. We would ask then that he who is convicted of fraudulent bankruptcy neither be permitted to continue his trade nor to engage in any new trade that may put him in a position to abuse public confidence, and that he even be banished with shame from the city. As to the unfortunate class [of real bankrupts], we ask that they be constrained to start paying off their debts from the moment their situation improves. . . .

10. These demands have led us little by little to the great tie that binds together all the parts of the kingdom, both internal and external, and by external I mean the colonies; The said tie has just been broken by a commercial treaty which, far from strengthening it, has completely destroyed it. The result has been that the specious attraction of a decrease in prices of a considerable number of materials suitable to our manufactures has impoverished men very necessary to the state; that is, the class of the poor. This cannot be denied, for everyday we see the poor man, so useful on account of the work he does, because he is the lynchpin of trade, the poor man, so useful to the service of the king because who among us, gentlemen, sacrifices himself so easily as the poor man signing up for eight years to defend

his country? One must admit that scarcely one in a hundred among the well off would be found to do so. Very well, gentlemen, this is the class whose destruction has begun as a result of the extreme poverty that pursues its members and which will end up destroying them, if the spread of machinery in France is not stopped.

It would be very nice to imitate our neighbors, even to surpass them in everything that perfects the arts. But there are social considerations: the survival of all the individuals who make up society. They form, under a good king, a single family, and they must supply one another with bread to feed that family. It is therefore an immutable fact that machines are not suitable in a great realm where so many hands would be forced to separate themselves from the body of the nation and to beg their livelihood from a foreigner who would ask nothing better than to enfeeble a nation that is inexhaustible in men and resources, a nation that has already spread throughout the universe but that would be exhausted by the desertion of this lower class which, perhaps too soon, may become German, Prussian, English or Russian. There are already examples of this too baleful for France, but they arose from other reasons which we will not recall because it always makes us shiver to do so. [This is an allusion to the emigration of Huguenots after the revocation of the Edict of Nantes in 1685.]

Depopulation, gentlemen, considered from every point of view never has any but terrible effects, but let that pass. Every man is capable of feeling it. Let us return to our main point which looks adversely upon machinery. Only a small number of men can run these great enterprises [in which machinery would be used] and even then they must be organized into companies. Certainly it is good that they will cut prices of manufactured goods, but wouldn't it be better to leave things as the are ... to let this large family suffice unto itself as it knew how to do before the commercial treaty existed, if the result is that the factory doors are surrounded by wretches crying out against the manufacturers for having cut off their arms, wretches who, in despair, will take refuge in the forests, will devastate the countryside, will stop people on the highways and will destroy the kingdom. This treaty broken, there will no longer be any competition for goods manufactured in the kingdom, consumed in the kingdom or in our colonies, because it will be of the greatest importance to prohibit the entry of all foreign merchandise and to enforce the prohibition by imposing the strictest penalties on lawbreakers. Then we will see joy reappear in everyone's heart which today is seen only among a few wealthy people who are in a position to bear up under the stress of the terrible events taking place every day. But let us not call the rich capitalists egoists: they are our brothers. Let us try to convince them, on the contrary, that they should unite with us for the general welfare, the source from which private welfare flows. . . .

We ought, gentlemen, to admire the industriousness of our capitalists who only had in mind the good they were inclined, and thought that they would be able, to do. Let us believe in the purity of their intentions. It is unfortunate that, by suppressing machinery, French goods will cost a little more than foreign ones but, as I've already noted, gentlemen, there will be no competition and no problems about markets.

Machinery was no doubt very suitable to the English. For what reason? The immensity of their trade on account of their great possessions in the colonies and North America, and the few goods they have for their subsistance. . . .

11. . . . Provincial Administration, although its title and members are worthy of respect, is not what is generally desired and, without going into any of the reasons that each man may have, it seems that what is wanted is the provincial estates. It is hoped that the estates will create an administration whose members will be elected by the assembled citizens without influence of protection or association of rank . . .

In order that this body may be considered the representative of the great province that must set it up, we believe that all groups indiscriminately ought to have members in it, beginning with the clergy, the nobility, the Parliament, the courts, the lawyers and other parts of the third estate, and artisans and merchants jointly appointed among all the ranks from the great traders to the artisan. As each must contribute to the burden of supporting the state and the people, the body ought to be competent to deal with the taxes that must necessarily be imposed on all the individuals of the province.

We have examples of the unity of feeling that exists in bodies thus composed, as the administration for poor relief. We are convinced that from an administration chosen in this manner there will flow a river of abundance, from which will be born the wealth of the state, the tranquility of the prince and the freedom of the subjects.

12. [Money must be found, through taxation, to pay for current expenses and the debt. A simple tax, like the land tax, is the best. The elimination of the bureaucracy of tax collection will save money].

If the land tax is assessed equally on all property indiscriminately, on property belonging to the clergy and nobility as well as in the third estate, receipts will increase by half, if not more. To this effect there must be no privileges or immunities that confer exemption from this tax. When the nation takes up arms it is for all the individuals who constitute it, and each must pay for the safekeeping that is provided him.

If the land tax thus assessed is not sufficient, another means, not at all onorous, can be found in the king's uncultivated domain land, which the crown may alienate. . . .

If these means did not suffice . . . the provincial estates, which are always ready to make sacrifices for their prince, could be called upon to vote a special subsidy in the form of a head tax. Even if this were only three livres per person, the population of the kingdom being estimated at twenty four millions this would provide an annual capital of seventy two millions. . . . And what individual, freed from the *aides*, the salt tax [and other indirect taxes] would not give this modest sum, when his prince will have rid him of the fetters that remain and which are so many plagues [upon the nation] at the same time as they are a considerable impedement to each person in particular. This extra-ordinary subsidy cannot fail to supply a very considerable sum, the more so as, through this form of taxation, all the individuals in the kingdom who do not own land will tax themselves in the guilds of which they are members in proportion to their means, in place of the land tax in whose burden they do not share.

33 FROM *Cahiers de Paroisses de l'Election du Blanc-en-Berry pour les Etats Généraux de 1789*

CAHIER DES DOLEANCES OF THE PARISH OF ST. GEORGES OF CIRON

The inhabitants of the parish, being extremely grateful to be able freely to enumerate the ways of lightening the burden of the taxes which the third estate alone has borne, and which was even heavier for

SOURCE. Yves Bohineust, *Les Cahiers de Paroisses de l'Election de Blanc-en-Berry pour les Etats Généraux de 1789* (Paris: Editions Les Presses Modernes, 1930), pp. 88–92. Translated for this volume by Susan Kaplow.

the poor because those of this estate who became rich could escape paying the large part which they would have been obliged to pay by buying noble titles.

The above, being desirous of acknowledging the benevolent intentions of His Majesty, charge their elected representatives to communicate to the assembly of Chateauroux the following:

1. That the state debts regarded as excessive be abolished.

2. That the ministers and their agents, both in the administration and in the treasury, have often established illegal taxes without the people's consent. That in the future, no taxes be levied except by the Estates General and that the aforesaid ministers be responsible for the sums they hold and also for their conduct in other matters.

3. That there be constituted a revenue sufficient to cover both the useful expenditures of the court and the interest on the national debt and that the burden of this be borne by each individual according to his ability.

4. That all privileges accorded on the basis of status be abolished and that the Estates General be constituted by individuals and not by orders.

5. That in each province of the realm provincial assemblies be constituted in which the third estate will be represented as in the Estates General. That these assemblies be accorded the power of ratifying taxes.

6. That the Parlements and other high judicial bodies be composed half of clergymen and nobles and half of individuals from the third estate; that justice be made more accesible to those subject to it.

7. That the *gabelle* (salt tax) be abolished—

   a. As revolting to humanity, since it causes citizens to cut each other's throats,

   b. As harmful to the population because the excessive price of salt deprives the poor of their best food.

   c. As detrimental to agriculture as it is thus deprived of a part of the labor it needs,

   d. Because it is the school of criminals and the source of crime.

There follows from this tax an abuse of the worst sort. It is contrary to natural law, greatly harasses traders, travelers, and inhabitants, and keeps the sick from getting the promptest relief, both spiritual and temporal, to which they are entitled. This abuse is the obligation imposed on all ferrymen on the canal to give their boats over to the Commis de Gabelles at sunset, being able to retrieve them only at sunrise.[1] The people, for the most part, can operate the boats only at great risk, and cannot do so at all when there is the least swelling. Thus many individuals are often deprived of religious ministrations and voyagers are greatly delayed.

8. That indirect taxes on trade be abolished since they greatly impede internal commerce.

9. That domain rights be simplified and certified so that every citizen may know what he owes.

10. That agriculture, the magistracy, the arts and commerce demand the return to their ranks of those ennobled in the last hundred years; that in the future, noble titles not be sold since this debases them; that only the soldier and the citizen of merit should have the right to a title. One likes to think that the ancient and good nobility will be pleased if its privileges are no longer cheapened.

11. That the *aides* and other duties in this category be reduced to a single duty if not abolished.

12. That feudalism be abolished without prejudice to the lords. That their honorary rights be maintained; that they be reimbursed the value, as estimated by an expert, of the duties such as the *banalité* and the *corvée in kind* which are so burdensome to the people and harmful to agriculture.

13. That a uniform legal code, system of weights and measures and, if possible, tax regime, be established. In any case, tax collection should be simplified.

14. That there be abolished Royal pensions gained through intrigue and all which are excessive and abusive, such as those given Comptrollers General of Finance who have not served at least ten years with distinction.

15. That it would be in the interest of economy to do away with the position of provincial governor inside the realm, or at least with the emoluments thereof.

16. That different projects tending to alter the uniforms or composition of the troops not be put so readily into effect. Changes only annoy the soldier and lead to desertion; they are also very expensive.

17. [That church properties be sold and the product of sale be assigned to the support of each individual of the said ecclesiastical order according to his utility, quality, rank, and dignity. That the surplus product be used to pay off the national debt.]

---

[1] The idea was to prevent contraband.

18. That the Berry and many other provinces would profit if the river Creuse were made navigable; these regions are deprived of all branches of commerce; this is bad for agriculture, and encourages indigence, the source of all evil.

19. That the ecclesiastical Seigneurs or, failing them, lay Seigneurs, should be obliged to provide for manufactures—this is the usual practice in most parishes but is not universal, adding to the burdens of which the poor feel all the weight.

20. That for the honor of religion, the *casuels*[2] of the priests be abolished. . . .

The community charges the aforesaid inhabitants to have adopted into the *cahiers* of Chateauroux and Bourges their wishes, grievances, complaints, and remonstrances.

Done and adopted, dictated and written, by us the undersigned on this fourth day of March, in the year of our Lord one thousand seven hundred and eighty-nine.

34 FROM   *Typical Cahiers of 1789*

CAHIER OF THE GRIEVANCES, COMPLAINTS AND REMONSTRANCES OF THE MEMBERS OF THE THIRD ESTATE OF THE BAILLIAGE OF VERSAILLES

Constitution

Art. 1. The power of making laws resides in the king and the nation.

Art. 2. The nation being too numerous for a personal exercise of this right, has confided its trust to representatives freely chosen from all classes of citizens. These representatives constitute the national assembly.

---

[2] *Casuels* were the payments made to a priest for certain services, e.g., baptism, marriage, burial, special masses.

SOURCE. Merrick Whitcomb, ed., *Typical Cahiers of 1789* in *University of Pennsylvania Translations and Reprints from the Original Sources of European History,* **IV** (1897), Number 5. pp. 23–36.

Art. 3. Frenchmen should regard as laws of the kingdom those alone which have been prepared by the national assembly and sanctioned by the king.

Art. 4. Succession in the male line and primogeniture are usages as ancient as the monarchy, and ought to be maintained and consecrated by solemn and irrevocable enactment.

Art. 5. The laws prepared by the States General and sanctioned by the king shall be binding upon all classes of citizens and upon all provinces of the kingdom. They shall be registered literally and accurately in all courts of law. They shall be open for consultation at all seats of municipal and communal government; and shall be read at sermon time in all parishes.

Art. 6. That the nation may not be deprived of that portion of legislation which is its due, and that the affairs of the kingdom may not suffer neglect and delay, the States General shall be convoked at least every two or three years.

Art. 7. No intermediate commission of the States General may ever be established, since deputies of the nation have no right to delegate the powers confirmed to them.

Art. 8. Powers shall be conferred upon delegates for one year only: but they may be continued or confirmed by a single re-election.

Art. 9. The persons of deputies shall be inviolable. They may not be prosecuted in civil cases during their term of office; nor held responsible to the executive authorities for any speech made in the assembly; but they shall be responsible to the States General alone.

Art. 10. Deputies of the Third Estate, or their president or speaker, shall preserve the same attitude and demeanor as the representatives of the two upper orders, when they address the sovereign. As regards the three orders there shall be no difference observed in the ceremonial made use of at the convocation of the estates.

Art. 11. Personal liberty, proprietary rights and the security of citizens shall be established in a clear, precise and irrevocable manner. All *lettres de cachet* shall be abolished forever, subject to certain modifications which the States General may see fit to impose.

Art. 12. And to remove forever the possibility of injury to the personal and proprietary rights of Frenchmen, the jury system shall be introduced in all criminal cases, and in civil cases for the determination of fact, in all the courts of the realm.

Art. 13. All persons accused of crimes not involving the death penalty shall be released on bail within twenty-four hours. This release shall be pronounced by the judge upon the decision of the jury.

Art. 14. All persons who shall have been imprisoned upon suspicion, and afterwards proved innocent, shall be entitled to satisfaction and damages from the state, if they are able to show that their honor or property has suffered injury.

Art. 15. A wider liberty of the press shall be accorded, with this provision alone: that all manuscripts sent to the printer shall be signed by the author, who shall be obliged to disclose his identity and bear the responsibility of his work; and to prevent judges and other persons in power from taking advantage of their authority, no writing shall be held a libel until it is so determined by twelve jurors, chosen according to the forms of a law which shall be enacted upon this subject.

Art. 16. Letters shall never be opened in transit; and effectual measures shall be taken to the end that this trust shall remain inviolable.

Art. 17. All distinctions in penalties shall be abolished; and crimes committed by citizens of the different orders shall be punished irrespectively, according to the same forms of law and in the same manner. The States General shall seek to bring it about that the effects of transgression shall be confined to the individual, and shall not be reflected upon the relatives of the transgressor, themselves innocent of all participation.

Art. 18. Penalties shall in all cases be moderate and proportionate to the crime. All kinds of torture, the rack and the stake, shall be abolished. Sentence of death shall be pronounced only for atrocious crimes and in rare instances, determined by the law.

Art. 19. Civil and criminal laws shall be reformed.

Art. 20. The military throughout the kingdom shall be subject to the general law and to the civil authorities, in the same manner as other citizens.

Art. 21. No tax shall be legal unless accepted by the representatives of the people and sanctioned by the king.

Art. 22. Since all Frenchmen receive the same advantage from the government, and are equally interested in its maintenance, they ought to be placed upon the same footing in the matter of taxation.

Art. 23. All taxes now in operation are contrary to these principles and for the most part vexations, oppressive and humiliating to the people. They ought to be abolished as soon as possible, and replaced by others common to the three orders and to all classes of citizens, without exception.

Art. 24. In case the present taxes are provisionally retained, it should be for a short time, not longer than the session of the States General, and it shall be ordered that the proportional contribution of the two upper orders shall be due from them on the day of the promulgation of the law of the constitution.

Art. 25. After the establishment of the new taxes, which shall be paid by the three orders, the present exceptional method of collecting from the clergy shall be done away with, and their future assemblies shall deal exclusively with matters of discipline and dogma.

Art. 26. All new taxes, real and personal, shall be established only for a limited time, never to exceed two or three years. At the expiration of this term, they shall be no longer collected, and collectors or other officials soliciting the same shall be proceeded against as guilty of extortion.

Art. 27. The anticipation of future revenues, loans in whatsoever disguise, and all other financial expedients of the kind, of which so great abuse has been made, shall be forbidden.

Art. 28. In case of war, or other exceptional necessity, no loan shall be made without the consent of the States General, and it shall be enacted that no loan shall be effected, without provision being made by taxation for the payment of interest, and of the principal at a specified time.

Art. 29. The amount which each citizen shall be obliged to pay, in case of war, by reason of an increase in the existing taxes, at a certain rate per livre, shall be determined beforehand by the States General in conjunction with the king. The certainty of increase ought to have a marked effect in preventing useless and unjust wars, since it clearly indicates to Frenchmen the new burden they will have to bear, and to foreign nations the resources which the nation has in reserve and at hand to repulse unjust attacks.

Art. 30. The exact debt of the government shall be established by the States General, and after verification it shall be declared the national debt.

Art. 31. Perpetual and life annuities shall be capitalized at their present value and discharged.

Art. 32. The expenses of the departments shall be determined by their actual needs, and so established by a committee of the States General, in such a manner that the expenditures may never exceed the sums appropriated.

Art. 33. There shall be no increase in taxation, until the receipts and expenditures have been compared with the utmost care, and a real deficit discovered; in fact, not until all possible reductions have been made in the expenses of each department.

Art. 34. The expenses of the war department call for the special attention of the States General. These expenses amount annually to the appalling sums of 110 and 120 millions. In order to effect their reduction, the States General shall demand the accounts of this department under the recent ministries, particularly under the ministry of the Duc de Choiseul.

Art. 35. The present militia system, which is burdensome, oppressive and humiliating to the people, shall be abolished; and the States General shall devise means for its reformation.

Art. 36. A statement of pensions shall be presented to the States General; they shall be granted only in moderate amounts, and then only for services rendered. The total annual expenditure for this purpose should not exceed a fixed sum. A list of pensions should be printed and made public each year.

Art. 37. Since the nation undertakes to provide for the personal expenses of the sovereign, as well as for the crown and state, the law providing for the inalienability of the domain shall be repealed. As a result, all parcels of the domain immediately in the king's possession, as well as those already pledged, and for the forests of His Majesty as well, shall be sold, and transferred in small lots, in so far as possible, and always at public auction to the highest bidder; and the proceeds applied to the reduction of the public debt. In the meanwhile all woods and forests shall continue to be controlled and administered, whoever may be the actual proprietors, according to the provisions of the law of 1669.

Art. 38. The execution of this law shall be confided to the provincial estates, which shall prosecute violations of the law before judges in ordinary.

Art. 39. Appanages shall be abolished and replaced, in the case of princes who possess them, with cash salaries, which shall be included in the expenses of the crown.

Art. 40. The States General shall take under advisement these transfers which have not yet been verified and completed.

Art. 40. b. Ministers and all government officials shall be responsible to the States General for their conduct of affairs. They may be impeached according to fixed forms of law and punished according to the statute.

Art. 41. All general and particular statements and accounts relative to the administration shall be printed and made public each year.

Art. 42. The coinage may not be altered without the consent of the Estates; and no bank established without their approval.

Art. 43. A new subdivision shall be made of the provinces of the realm; provincial estates shall be established, members of which, not excepting their presidents, shall be elected.

Art. 44. The constitution of the provincial estates shall be uniform throughout the kingdom, and fixed by the States General. Their powers shall be limited to the interior administration of the provinces, under the supervision of His Majesty, who shall communicate to them the national laws which have received the consent of the States General and the royal sanction: to which laws all the provincial estates shall be obliged to submit without reservation.

Art. 45. All members of the municipal assemblies of towns and villages shall be elected. They may be chosen from all classes of citizens. All municipal offices now existing shall be abolished; and their redemption shall be provided for by the States General.

Art. 46. All offices and positions, civil, ecclesiastical and military, shall be open to all orders; and no humiliating and unjust exceptions (in the case of the third estate), destructive to emulation and injurious to the interests of the state, shall be perpetuated.

Art. 47. The right of *aubaine* shall be abolished with regard to all nationalities. All foreigners, after three years' residence in the kingdom, shall enjoy the rights of citizenship.[1]

Art. 48. Deputies of French colonies in America and in the Indies, which form an important part of our possessions, shall be admitted to the States General, if not at the next meeting, at least at the one following.

Art. 49. All relics of serfdom, agrarian or personal, still remaining in certain provinces, shall be abolished.

Art. 50. New laws shall be made in favor of the Negroes in our colonies; and the States General shall take measures towards the abolition of slavery. Meanwhile let a law be passed, that Negroes in the colonies who desire to purchase their freedom, as well as those whom their masters are willing to set free, shall no longer be compelled to pay a tax to the domain.

Art. 51. The three functions, legislative, executive and judicial, shall be separated and carefully distinguished.

The communes[2] of the bailliage of Versailles have already expressed

[1] The *Droit d'Aubaine* was the right attributed to the king to inherit the property of foreigners who died in France. This applied, of course, only to property *in* France. Nevertheless, it was acknowledged to be totally unreasonable, a hindrance to trade, and it was the subject of numerous treaties between France and the major European states, so that it was not much invoked at the end of the old regime.

[2] The communes, i.e., the Third Estate.

themselves in respect to the necessity of adopting the form of deliberation *per capita* in the coming States General. The reform of the constitution will be one of their principal duties. This magnificent monument of liberty and public felicity should be the work of the three orders in common session; if they are separated, certain pretensions, anxieties and jealousies are bound to arise; the two upper orders are likely to oppose obstacles, perhaps invincible, to the reform of abuses and the enactment of laws destined to suppress such abuses. It seems indispensable that in this first assembly votes should be taken *per capita* and not by order. After the renunciation by the upper two orders of their pecuniary privileges; after all distinctions before the law have been abolished; when the exclusion of the third estate from certain offices and positions has been done away with,—then the reasons which to-day necessitate deliberation *per capita* will no longer exist.

The communes of Versailles therefore refrain from expressing a positive opinion upon the future composition of the national assemblies and upon the method of their deliberation. They defer, with all confidence, the decision of this important question to the wisdom of the States General.

Our prayer is that the methods determined upon shall be such as will assure forever, to the king and to the nation, those portions of the legislative power which respectively belong to them; that they shall maintain between them a perfect equilibrium in the employment of this power; that they shall conserve, forever, to the nation its rights and liberties; to the king his prerogatives and the executive power in all its fulness. Finally that these methods should be so combined as to produce that circumspectness and lack of haste so necessary to the enactment of laws, and that they will effectually prevent all hasty counsels, dissentions amongst deputies and immature conclusions.

May all deputies to this august assembly, impressed with the sanctity and extent of their obligations, forget that they are the mandatories of some special order, and remember only that they are representatives of the people. May they never be forgetful of the fact, that they are about to fix the destinies of the foremost nation of the world!

The Executive

Art. 52. It shall be ordained by the constitution that the executive power be vested in the king alone.

Art. 53. The king shall dispose of all offices, places and positions, ecclesiastical, civil and military, to which he has at present the right of appointment.

Art. 54. All the provincial estates, or commissions representing them, shall receive his immediate orders, which it shall be their duty to obey provisionally.

Art. 55. His consent shall be necessary to all bills approved by the States General in order that they may acquire the force of law throughout the realm. He may reject all bills presented to him, without being obliged to state the reasons of his disapproval.

Art. 56. He shall have the sole right of convening, prorogueing and dissolving the States General.

The Judiciary

Art. 57. The sale of the judicial office shall be suppressed as soon as circumstances will permit, and provision made for the indemnification of holders.

Art. 58. There shall be established in the provinces as many superior courts as there are provincial estates. They shall be courts of final jurisdiction.

Art. 59. All exceptional and privileged seignorial courts shall be abolished, as well as other courts rendered useless by the abolition of certain taxes which causes their erection, and by the adoption of a new system of accounts under the exclusive control of the States General.

Art. 60. All rights of *committimus* or of evocation, which tend to favor certain classes of citizens to the detriment of the general public, shall be abolished.[3]

Art. 61. There shall be only two stages of jurisdiction.

Art. 62. Since the adoption of the jury system will have a tendency to facilitate and simplify the administration of justice, all classes of judges shall be reduced to the least number possible.

Art. 63. Each judge of the lower courts and of the superior provincial courts shall be appointed by the king out of a list of three candidates, presented by the provincial estates.

---

[3] *Committimus* was the right enjoyed by certain nobles and officers of the crown to have cases, in which they appeared as either plaintiff or defendant, heard by a higher court than would otherwise be the case. It applied only in civil matters and was a means by which the powerful could give legal color to a whole series of abuses.

Art. 64. Judges of all courts shall be obliged to adhere to the letter of the law, and may never be permitted to change, modify or interpret it at their pleasure.

Art. 65. The fees received by all officers of justice shall be fixed at a moderate rate and clearly understood; and judges who extort fees in excess of the fixed rates shall be condemned to pay a fine of four times the amount they have received.

Such are the bases of a constitution founded upon the eternal principles of justice and reason, which alone ought to regulate henceforward the government of the realm. Once they are adopted, all false pretensions, and all burdensome privileges, all abuses of all kinds will be seen to disappear. Already a considerable number of *bailliages* have expressed their desires concerning the reforms and abolitions to be effected in all branches of the administration; the necessity for these drastic changes has been so evident that it is sufficient merely to indicate them.

General Demands

Art. 66. The deputies of the *prévôté* and *vicomté* of Paris shall be instructed to unite themselves with the deputies of other provinces, in order to join with them in securing, as soon as possible, the following abolitions:

Of the *taille* ;
Of the *gabelle* ;
Of the *aides* ;
Of the *corvée* ;
Of the *ferme* of tobacco;
Of the registry-duties;
Of the free-hold tax;
Of the taxes on leather;
Of the government stamp upon iron;
Of the stamps upon gold and silver;
Of the interprovincial customs duties;
Of the taxes upon fairs and markets;

Finally, of all taxes that are burdensome and oppressive, whether on account of their nature or of the expense of collection, or because they have been paid almost wholly by agriculturists and by the poorer classes. They shall be replaced with other taxes, less complicated and easier of collection, which shall fall alike upon all classes and orders of the state without exception.

Art. 67. We demand also the abolition of the royal preserves [*capitaineries*];

Of the game laws;

Of jurisdictions of *prévôtés*;

Of *banalités*;

Of tolls;

Of useless authorities and governments in cities and provinces.

Art. 68. We solicit the establishment of public granaries in the provinces, under the control of the provincial estates, in order that by accumulating reserves during years of plenty, famine and excessive dearness of grain, such as we have experienced in the past, may be prevented.

Art. 69. We solicit also the establishment of free schools in all country parishes.

Art. 70. We demand, for the benefit of commerce, the abolition of all exclusive privileges:

The removal of customs barriers to the frontiers;

The most complete freedom in trade;

The revision and reform of all laws relative to commerce;

Encouragement for all kinds of manufacture, viz.: premiums, bounties and advances;

Rewards to artisans and laborers for useful inventions.

The communes desire that prizes and rewards shall always be preferred to exclusive privileges, which extinguish emulation and lessen competition.

Art. 71. We demand the suppression of various hindrances, such as stamps, special taxes, inspections; and the annoyances and visitations, to which many manufacturing establishments, particularly tanneries, are subjected.

Art. 72. The states General are entreated to devise means for abolishing guild organizations, indemnifying the holders of masterships; and to fix by the law the conditions under which the arts, trades and professions may be followed without the payment of an admission tax, and at the same time to provide that public security and confidence be undisturbed.

Art. 73. Deputies shall solicit the abolition of:

Receivers of consignments;

Pawn-brokers;

All lotteries;

The bank of Poissy;[4]

All taxes, of whatsoever nature, on grain and flour;

All franchises and exemptions enjoyed by post-agents, except a pecuniary indemnity which shall be accorded them;

The exclusive privilege of the transportation companies, which shall be allowed to continue their public service, in competition, however, with all private companies, which shall see fit to establish public carriages; and these, moreover, shall be encouraged.

Art. 74. They shall demand complete freedom of transport for grain among the various provinces of the kingdom, without interference from any court whatsoever.

Art. 75. They shall demand also the total abolition of all writs of suspension and of safe conducts.

Art. 76. Superior courts shall be absolutely prohibited from arresting, in any manner whatsoever, by means of decrees or decisions obtained upon petitions not made public, the execution of notarial writs or the decisions of judges of original jurisdiction, when the law shall ordain their provisional execution; under penalty that the judge shall be responsible for the amount of the debt, payment of which he had caused to be arrested.

Art. 77. The abolition of all places of refuge for debtors.

Art. 78. That no merchant or trader may be admitted to any national assembly or any municipal body, who has demanded abatement from his creditors; still less if he is a fraudulent bankrupt; and he may not be re-established in his rights until he has paid the whole amount of his indebtedness.

Art. 79. That individuals who have issued promissory notes shall be liable to detention.

Art. 80. That the States General shall consider means of diminishing mendicancy.

Art. 81. That civil and military offices may not be held simultaneously by the same person, and that each citizen may hold only one office.

Art. 82. That all the honorary rights of nobles shall be maintained; but that they shall be allowed to hunt only upon their own lands, and not upon the lands of their vassals or tenants.

---

[4] The *Caisse* (bank) of Poissy financed the purchases of meat by retail butchers through a system of loans. It was often blamed for creating artificial shortages or helping to raise the price of meat.

Art. 83. That nobility may be acquired neither through office nor by purchase.

Art. 84. That inheritances shall be divided equally among co-heritors of the same degree, without regard to sex or right of primogeniture, nor to the status of the co-participants, and without distinction between nobles and non-nobles.

Art. 85. That all entails shall be limited to one generation.

Art. 86. That day laborers may not be taxed to exceed the amount of one day's labor.

Art. 87. That there shall be established in all towns and country parishes commissions of arbitration, composed of a certain number of citizens elected and renewed annually, to which persons may apply and secure provisional judgment, without expense, except in case of appeal to the regular courts.

Art. 88. That all state prisons shall be abolished, and that means shall be taken to put all other prisons in better sanitary condition.

Art. 89. That it may please the States General to provide means for securing a uniformity of weights and measures throughout the kingdom.

Art. 90. That the laws upon *lods* and *ventes* shall be examined and rendered uniform throughout the kingdom.[5]

Art. 91. That parishes shall be furnished with power to redeem the tax upon the transfer of land.

Art. 92. That *dîmes* shall be suppressed and converted into a money rent based upon the price of corn and of the mark of silver, rising proportionately with the combined increase in value of corn and of the mark of silver.

Art. 93. Since clergymen in general ought not to occupy themselves with wordly affairs, there ought to be provided for bishops, archbishops and all holders of benefices a decent income and one suitable to their dignity; accordingly the property of the church in each province ought to be sold under the supervision of the provincial estates, which shall assume the duty of paying to holders of benefices the sums accorded to them by the States General.

Art. 94. That in case the above change should not be made, then it shall be ordained that no clergyman may hold two benefices at the same time, and that all persons now possessing two or more benefices

[5] *Lods et Ventes* was a seigneurial transfer tax due when a piece of land dependant on the lord's holdings was sold or otherwise changed hands. The amount varied from one-sixth to one-twelfth of the purchase price.

shall be obliged to choose and to declare, within a prescribed time, which one of them they desire to retain.

Art. 95. That all commendatory abbacies, benefices without functions and useless convents shall be suppressed, their possessions sold for the benefit of the state, and the funds thus realized made to constitute an endowment, the income of which shall be used for the benefit of country parish priests, for the establishment of free schools, hospitals and other charitable institutions.

Art. 96. That continuous residence of archbishops and bishops in their dioceses and of beneficiaries in their benefices shall be required; and that resignations be not permitted.

Art. 97. That no clergyman under the age of twenty-five may be promited to a sub-diaconate.

Art. 98. That girls may not enter religious orders until after they are twenty-five years of age, nor men until after thirty.

Art. 99. That it be forbidden to go to the Roman Curia for provisions, nominations, bulls and dispensations of all kinds; and each bishop in his diocese shall have full powers in these matters.

Art. 100. That the right of the pope to grant livings in France be suppressed.

Art. 101. That the Concordat be revoked, and all intervention on the part of the Roman Curia be made to cease.

Art. 102. That loans, contracted by the clergy to cover their contribution to the taxes which they were bound to support, shall be paid by them, since these loans are the obligation of the order; but loans which have been contracted on the government's account shall be included in the royal debt, and added to the national debt.

Various Matters

Art. 1. Deputies of the *prévôté-vicomté* shall be instructed to demand increased pay for soldiers.

Art. 2. That inhabitants of towns and rural places be paid and idemnified for troops of war quartered upon them, for the transportation of troops and of military baggage.

Art. 3. That the ordinances concerning the king's guard be revised, particularly those clauses which abolish the wise provision of Louis XIV. for the safety of his person, and the regulations made by him relative to his body-guard.

Art. 4. That barbarous punishments, taken from the codes of foreign nations and introduced into the new military regulations, be abolished, and replaced with regulations more in conformity with the genius of the nation.

(*Articles 5, 6 and 7 relate to notarial and registry fees.*)

Art. 8. That it be permitted to contract loans by means of bills or short-term certificates of debt, bearing interest at the legal rate, without it being necessary to alienate the capital so pledged.

Art. 9. In case the property of the church be not sold, that leases shall be continued by the successors of the present holders; at least that they shall not suffer a reduction of more than one-third.

Art. 10. That canals be constructed in all provinces of the kingdom where they will be useful.

Art. 11. That the working of mines be encouraged.

Art. 12. That a new schedule be made of the expenses of funerals, marriages and other church functions.

Art. 13. That cemetries be located outside of cities, towns and villages; that the same be done with places of deposit for refuse.

Art. 14. That the funds for the support of the lazarettos, formerly located in rural parishes, having been united with the endowments of hospitals, country people shall be permitted to send their sick to the city hospitals.

Art. 15. That the laws of the kingdom shall be equally the laws of the French colonies.

Art. 16. That all kinds of employment suitable for women shall be reserved for them by special enactment.

SUGGESTIONS FOR FURTHER READING

Barber, Elinor G., *The Bourgeoisie in 18th Century France* (Princeton, 1955).

Bloch, Marc, *French Rural History* (Berkeley, 1967).

Bluche, J. François, *Les Magistrats du Parlement de Paris au XVIIIe Siècle, 1715–1771* (Paris, 1960).

Cobb, Richard, *Police and the French Popular Protest, 1789–1820* (Oxford, 1970).

Coornaert, Emile, *Les Corporations en France avant 1789* (Paris, second edition 1968).

Coornaert, Emile, *Les Compagnonnages* (Paris, 1967).

Couturier, Marcel, *Recherches sur les Structures Sociales de Chateaudun, 1525–1789* (Paris, 1969).

Ford, Franklin, *Robe and Sword: The Regrouping of the French Aristocracy after Louis XIV* (Cambridge, Mass., 1953).

Hufton, Olwen H., *Bayeux in the Late Eighteenth Century, A Social Study* (Oxford, 1967).

Kaplow, Jeffry, *Elbeuf During the Revolutionary Period, 1770–1815: History and Social Structure* (Baltimore, 1964).

Kaplow, Jeffry, *The Parisian Laboring Poor on the Eve of the Revolution* (New York, forthcoming 1971).

Labrousse, C.E., *La Crise de l'Économie Française à la Fin de l'Ancien Régime et au Debut de la Révolution* (Paris, 1944).

Lefebvre, Georges, *The Coming of the French Revolution* (Princeton, 1947, trans. R.R. Palmer).

Lefebvre, Georges, *Etudes Orléanasises* (Paris, two volumes, 1962–63).

Lefebvre, Georges, *The French Revolution* (New York, two volumes, 1959–62).

Lefebvre, Georges, *Les paysans du Nord pendant la Révolution Française* (Paris, two volumes, 1924).

Le Roy Ladurie, Emmanuel, *Les paysans du Languedoc* (Paris, 1966).

Méthivier, Hubert, *L'ancien régime* (Paris, 1961).

Meyer, Jean, *La Noblesse Bretonne au XVIIIe Siècle* (Paris, two volumes, 1966).

Poitrineau, Abel, *La Vie Rurale en Basse-Auvergne a XVIIIe Siècle.* (Paris, two volumes, 1965).

Robin, Régine, *La Société Française en 1789: Semur-en-Auxois* (Paris, 1970).

Saint-Jacob, P. de, *Les Paysans de la Bourgogne du Nord* (Paris, 1964).

Senton, J., *Fortunes et groupes sociaux à Toulouse sous la Révolution, 1789–1799* (Toulouse, 1969).

Soboul, Albert, *La Révolution Française* (Paris, two volumes, 1964).

Tocqueville, Alexis de, *The Old Regime and the Revolution* (New York, 1955; originally published 1856).

Vaissière, Pierre de, *Gentilshommes Campagnards de l'Ancienne France* (Paris, third edition, 1903).

Young, Arthur (ed. J. Kaplow), *Travels in France during the Years 1787–1788–1789* (New York, 1969; originally published 1792).